LIVE ART ON CAMERA:
PERFORMANCE AND PHOTOGRAPHY

Edited by
Alice Maude-Roxby

John Hansard Gallery

Published on the occasion of the exhibition:

'Live Art on Camera'

John Hansard Gallery
Southampton, 18 September – 10 November 2007

Exhibition curated and publication edited by Alice Maude-Roxby
Project co-ordination by Ros Carter
Installation photography by Steve Shrimpton
Publication and exhibition panels designed by Sarah Backhouse

'Live Art on Camera' has been organised by
John Hansard Gallery

Exhibition and research financially supported by:
Arts Council England, Sheffield Hallam University, Arts and
Humanities Research Council, The Elephant Trust.

Published by John Hansard Gallery
University of Southampton, Southampton SO17 1BJ, UK
www.hansardgallery.org.uk
tel: 02380 592158
fax: 02380 594192
email: hansard@soton.ac.uk

Printed by Creative Press London
Distributed by Cornerhouse Publications, Manchester UK.
ISBN: 978 085432 875 8

The John Hansard Gallery is supported by Arts Council England and University of
Southampton.

Front cover photograph: *Reporters from the American LIFE magazine photographing
Shiraga Kazuo participating in the "One-Day-Only Outdoor Exhibition (Ruins
Exhibition)" at the Yoshihara Oil Mill Nishinomiya Refinery, April 1956.*
Photographer unknown. ©: The former members of the Gutai Art Association.
Courtesy: Ashiya City Museum of Art & History.

CONTENTS

The John Hansard Gallery would like to extend warm and sincere thanks
to all of the artists and photographers who are represented in the exhibition,
their help and enthusiasm for the project has proved invaluable.

We would also like to express our extreme gratitude to the following
individuals and organisations who have helped towards the realisation of this
project:–

Elaine McElroy; Milly Glimcher, Pace Wildenstein Gallery, New York; Lois
Keidan, Live Arts Development Agency; Lisa Watts; Anna Harding; Barbara
Moore; Laure Leber; Mary Sabbatino, Galerie Lelong, New York; Thomas
Erben Gallery, New York; Dr Elisabeth Klotz and Dr Susanne Märtens, the
Adrian Piper Research Archive, Berlin; Shuzo Fujiwara and Kato Mizuho,
Ashiya City Museum, Ashiya, Japan; Kodaira Masahiro and Ohtsuji Seiko,
Ohtsuji Kiyoji Estate; Jen Stamp, Carolee Schneemann archive; Andrea
Mardegan; Brian Liddy and Ruth Kitchin, National Media Museum, Bradford;
Dr Stephan von Wiese and Mattijs Visser, Kunstpalast Dusseldorf; Ben Cook
and Jackie Holt, LUX, London; Theus Zwakhals, Montevideo, Amsterdam;
Robert Panzer, VAGA; Roy Willingham, Paintworks, London; Michael
Dyer, London; John Deaville, London; Barbara Clausen; Kathy O'Dell;
Carrie Lambert-Beatty; Margarethe Clausen; Takako Jin; Andrea Mardegan;
Arts Council England; Sheffield Hallam University; Arts and Humanities
Research Council; The Elephant Trust; Adeline Guy, Oxford Exhibition
Services; Julian Grater; Josef Pluhar.

Special thanks go to Joan Giroux for her dedication to this project throughout
its development and for her careful proofing and improvement of the texts.

Grateful thanks also to fellow staff at John Hansard Gallery: Adrian Hunt,
Nicky Balfour, Ronda Gowland, Nicky Anderson, Vic Anderson, Ratna Bibi,
Liz Jones, Naomi McGrew, Jenny Gipaki and Joel Papps.

During the 1960s the most significant development in radical art practice was the tendency for artists to challenge the dominance of the commercial art market by increasingly making art that was temporary, transient, or ephemeral. One of the interesting facets of art practice since that time has been the relationship between the two interrelated fields of the non-art object and the commercial art market. In the immediate aftermath of its genesis, the notion of what constituted an art object began to change radically, and often it was the ephemera, document, or record that became the object to be exploited commercially. Sometimes artists are driven by a desire to protect their own creative process and sometimes by a desire to take control of their commercial viability. Often the phenomenon we think of as 'art' exists between the event and the object. Meanwhile, the marketplace itself shifts its position in order to maximise its commercial viability.

In recent years as the means of communication and documentation have become increasingly dependent on digital technology, a further shift has occurred. The nature of the archive itself is under challenge in an age where the requirement for speed and breadth has overtaken the need for precision and durability.

These twin concerns have been an almost ever-present concern running through the programming of the John Hansard Gallery for many years, and the resulting investigations have been extremely rich and rewarding. They explore a vital history of art from recent decades that challenges and provides a context for many younger artists working today. At the same time they also examine the nature of primary source material and its possible use for scholarship and research for future generations.

Perhaps the subject that most epitomises this twin concern is the relationship between a performance (arguably the most ephemeral of all art production) and its documentation through photography. Such a fecund area of investigation could lead to a much larger range of exemplars both cited within this publication and presented within the related exhibition. Invariably some key works in this larger project have been omitted. However, the examples presented constitute a narrative to explore the wider phenomenon.

Central to the theme is the issue of the relationship between artist and photographer. At its heart, the document of a performance is not the work, and neither is it a document; in every case it holds a position somewhere between the two, but there is no simple spectrum upon which a particular example can sit at a specific point. The relationship is far more complex, and in fact resembles a matrix rather than a spectrum. This complexity naturally challenges sensitivities of both artist and photographer, and we are extremely grateful for the generosity and support of both in the development of this project.

Given the transient nature of the material that forms the basis of the exhibition, such material is often more precious than the rare art object that it may originally have sought to replace. We are therefore deeply indebted to all those who agreed to lend objects and materials for the exhibition.

Finally, I would like to express my thanks to Alice Maude-Roxby, who edited this publication and conceived of the exhibition to which it relates. Her diligence and intelligence make sense of an extremely complex subject. Her approach creates a benchmark that will prove seminal in the further work that will undoubtedly take place in the future.

Stephen Foster
Director
John Hansard Gallery

LIVE ART ON CAMERA: AN INTRODUCTION

Alice Maude-Roxby
August 2007

The exhibition *Live Art on Camera* has evolved from a series of discussions on the subject of performance documentation. These conversations have taken place in artists', photographers', and filmmakers' studios and archives. The impetus was to learn more about the ways in which our reading of seminal performances, through performance documentation, has potentially been influenced through the intentions, ideas, and aesthetics of those who recorded the events. I became interested in the various renditions photographers and artists gave, often many years after the event, in which their descriptions fused the content of a performance both to the cultural context of its time and to the process of its making. Speaking in retrospect and in reference to specifics of the times in which these works were made, underlying social and political contexts to which the works often made direct reference were brought to the fore. Photographs were discussed regarding both what was depicted and what might be missing or what had not been recorded, moments that happened immediately before or after the event. Also discussed were the trajectories of how performance photographs and films had circulated and were distributed through inclusion in different publications, screenings, and exhibitions.

Meetings took place in various archives: locations ranging from museums, bank vaults, studios, or kitchens to bedrooms reflected the extremely varying values placed on these documents. On some days I saw documentation of the same piece in two or three archives, at times wearing or not wearing white gloves as prints were variously retrieved from meticulously arranged filing systems, or dusted and wiped down after being pulled out of boxes stored in lofts or cellars. Within the contexts of these different archives, I saw documentation of seminal performances immersed in entirely different image contexts that are individualistic and characteristic of each photographer's or artist's ongoing practice. In retrospect, my experience of seeing the performance photographs in this fashion reminded me of the process of reading image sequences in Aby Warburg's *Picture Atlas Mnemosyne* panels (1924–1929).[1] In this work collections of diverse images from very different sources that share subject reference are read in relation to each other, without individual captions. Within the photographers' archives I often noted surprising similarities within image compositions as well as how the body had been framed

Aby Warburg, *Mnemosyne Atlas, Panel 60: Schilderhebung, morris dancing, tossing in the air*, 1928–29. Photograph courtesy of the Warburg Institute, London.

across several portfolios of work, widening a sense of how photographic styles and conventions are characteristic of broader cultural and temporal influences. Diverse portfolios were sometimes linked by an evident photographic style, connecting the performance photographs to entirely different image contexts. At other times there seemed little stylistic connection but rather a social or cultural common ground adding to an understanding of the underlying conceptual content of a performance and its relationship to contemporary culture.

The exhibition *Live Art on Camera* forefronts the activities and intentions of filmmakers and photographers who have documented a selection of performances in Japan, Europe, and the United States since the 1950s. This is manifested, for purposes of the exhibition, either by physically situating those performance documents next to examples of the same photographer's or filmmaker's practice, or through the invitation to artists and photographers to make new works through which the process of recording performance and aspects of attributes characteristic of performance photographs can be examined. I asked artists to examine how their performances have been translated through the work of various photographers or filmmakers, and asked photographers and filmmakers to reflect on their experiences of recording performance, their intentions, and the relationship of these performance documents to the wider context of their ongoing practices. In shifting emphasis from one side of the camera to the other; from the lived experience and intentions of the artist pictured to the lived experience and intentions of the photographer or filmmaker, present and experiencing the work through the camera, the content of the work is temporarily more evidently anchored within the nuts and bolts of the process of its recording.

The initial impetus to examine the various ways performance has been recorded through an analysis of the recording photographer's or filmmaker's ongoing practice came through a fascination with documentation of Gina Pane's actions in the 1970s. The hook that caught me was the jarring convergence of the content of the actions in which Pane was photographed with certain photographic attributes more usually associated with commercial photography. In full colour, high focus, and very carefully (and often centrally) composed images, gestures characteristic of Pane's high-risk performance (the insertion of thorns into her arm, the eating of raw meat, the drinking and spitting out of milk, the cutting of her flesh) are conveyed. Upon closer view it becomes evident that some of the works documented with a live audience present were photographically lit, and the unfolding of the actions required that the photographer move in close

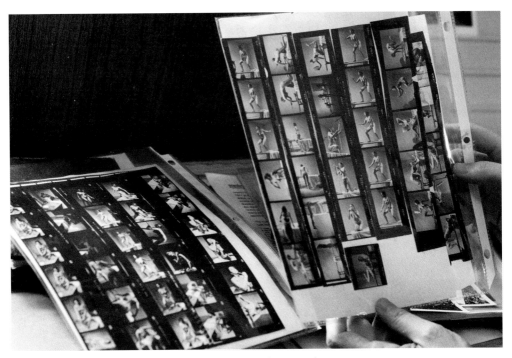

Schneemann Studio, New Paltz, NY, 2006, photograph © Jennifer Kotter.

Kurt Kren, Stills from *10B/65 Silber-Aktion Brus*, 1965. Photographs courtesy of LUX, London.

to the artist to achieve the shots. Gina Pane meticulously planned her actions and instructed photographer Françoise Masson as to the photographs she should take. The fact that Pane employed the same photographer over ten years and that a particular photographic style is so fused to the work compelled me to track down Françoise Masson to ask about her experience of the actions.[2] Seeing her photographs of Pane in the context of her commercial photography opened up my understanding of the implications of photographic style on performance and further fuelled my intrigue to investigate the incredibly varying modes in which performance has been recorded.

The levels of engagement and intentionality with which photographers have approached the task of recording live art ranges from individuals for whom the role is a one-off spontaneously generated act to those who have absolutely committed to the activity as a specialism, in some cases a specialism of solely recording live art over decades. The spectrum of images produced ranges from a seemingly anonymous, apparently objective documentary representation to a highly subjective translation where the application of a particular style is present. In these cases, it is difficult in retrospect to disassociate the photographer's signature from the look of the work of the artist pictured. This is particularly true, for example in the case of Kurt Kren's documentations of Otto Muehl and Gunter Brus where dense editing results in a frame that jumps from one viewpoint to another, and the extreme changes in the way light is recorded–from burnt-out overexposure to underexposure–have become fused to the work, influencing how the content of the action is subsequently understood. Kren planned the structure of the film in advance, drawing on graph paper a numbered system of frames and edits, enabling him to edit 'in the camera' whilst filming. Regarding the influence of Kren on the work of the Actionists, Otto Muehl said, 'Kurt Kren deserves to be mentioned in the same breath as the protagonists of early Viennese Actionsim'.[3] Kren's performance films, and the attributes of time, structure, and light that he explored within them, however, are an episode within an experimental film career begun before and much further expanded upon in his

Kurt Kren, Still from *3/60 Baume im Herbst*, 1960. Photograph courtesy of LUX, London.
Hollis Frampton, Still from *Lemon*, 1969. Photograph courtesy of LUX, London.

subsequent non-performance structuralist films.

Artist Hollis Frampton consistently photographed Carl Andre's early sculptures from 1958 to 1962. In retrospect Frampton wrote:

> I didn't find it a picnic to be a photographer, through the sixties, not because photography was disregarded, although of course that was true, but because my predicament was that of a committed illusionist in an environment that was officially dedicated to the eradication of illusion.[4]

Regarding his view of photography in relation to art, Andre is quoted, 'Art is a direct experience with something in the world, and photography is just a rumour, a kind of pornography of art.'[5] Whilst this viewpoint may not seem surprising in relation to the emphasis on materiality characteristic of the practice of artists like Carl Andre, it is interesting to consider that an artist as radical as John Cage was also highly suspicious of the reductivist quality of reproduction, refusing to own phonographs of music. Andre saw as a loss and process of diminution that through the recording process his sculptures were 'reduced' to small flat black and white photographs. Frampton, on the other hand, saw the conceptual potential of this deadpan view: static objects changed through a process of reproduction, and the manner in which they have been framed up by the camera. Perhaps this change in the reading of an object is closer to the appropriation of found objects inserted as art within conceptualism, a position borne out by Frampton's later work as a filmmaker. Frampton said:

> I didn't want to announce or to give out as something that I had done, something that showed the direct signature, the imprint of my having without mediation manipulated it. I liked to do things with machines so I took up still photography which seemed to offer that advantage, that of mediation, that of signaturelessness, of a certain kind at least. The signature was in such things as framing and tonal scalings, abstractions as imperceptible as the infinitely thin clean line. So that one was not, as it were, the person hovering behind the artifact but rather behind the thing that made the artifact. And on the other hand, one did not have to

laboriously build up this image. It was not made serially but came forward as a kind of matrix of thought instantaneously, in a manner that criticised the matter.[6]

Within his four-minute film *Lemon*, Frampton positions and moves lights in relation to a centrally framed lemon. The resulting change in light is systematically recorded to a climax. In relation to the lemon, the illumination proceeds with the same drama and effect of an eclipse of the sun, whilst the lemon occupies space in a static orbit. This mundane presentation of the lemon is essential to contrast with the drama created by the choreographed lighting.

Sometimes recording styles seem fused to the time in which they were made. In the case of Joseph Beuys, comparing photographs published during his lifetime to those published since his death demonstrates how his works seem to have changed from being predominantly represented by black and white, often slightly out of focus, or with a low depth of field grainy photographs, to those which seem more closely to fit the criteria of a 'technically good' image.[7] Regarding the embracement of colour since Beuys' death Caroline Tisdall, one photographer who consistently photographed his actions, reflects:

> When Beuys died everybody really started to use colour. They started using colour for *Palazzo Regale,* the last big work. It was just a mode, not a fashion, but a way of seeing the work. When asked why he used so much grey with the felt, Beuys once said, "Well I do it because there is so much colour in the world". The atmosphere of the work always seemed to me to be black and white. I started to take colour photographs before he died, and they don't have the same resonance.[8]

The transcripts collected here expose aspects of changing perceptions of both performance and photography within contemporary culture and contribute to debates about the impetus for the making, the experiencing, and the assimilating of art. Babette Mangolte, who extensively documented early works by Yvonne Rainer and Trisha Brown, situates her disaffection and ultimate end of photographing performance at a point in the early 1980s when artists began asking her to shoot publicity photos and headshots.[9] This fact compares interestingly to the position of contemporary photographers Hugo Glendinning and Manuel Vason who prefer to photograph performance art outside of the live event. Both Glendinning and Vason have taken on collaborative positions, Glendinning with Forced Entertainment and Vason, who shoots performance to camera with individual artists as a preferable mode of photographing performance rather than 'straight' documentation made at live events.

This difference in approach informs the changing considerations of the actuality of performance and of 'authenticity' in relation to public performances today. It opens up a consideration of the significance of photographic documentation as it has changed from the nature of a relic (where the action took place once) to part of a practice, which incorporates representation of performance within it. These wider changes since the 1960s regarding the relationship of photography to performance are issues certain artists have mediated within the trajectory of their own practices. Evident within Allan Kaprow's practice one sees a shift from photographs of public Happenings to a very particular 'instructional' style of photography where an action, repeatable by the viewer, is demonstrated to camera. This disaffection with Happenings documentation had to do with the fact that the physicality of the events seemed poorly represented through photographs, and additionally with the dynamic that as soon as photographers were present, participants began behaving 'as actors'.[10]

Footnotes

1. In Warburg's last panels, compiled in 1929 he combined contemporary 'non-art' visual material: see Charlotte Schoell-Glass, ' "Serious Issues": The Last Plates of Warburg's Picture Atlas Mnemosyne' published in Richard Woodfield, *Art History as Cultural History: Warburg's Projects*, G+B Arts International, 2001, pp. 183–202.

2. Gina Pane made drawings in which she planned aspects of the actions and discussed these with the photographer in advance of the event. Françoise Masson speaks about their process in *On Record: Advertising, Architecture and the Actions of Gina Pane*, Alice Maude-Roxby and Françoise Masson, Artwords Press, 2004.

3. Malcolm Green, *Brus, Muehl, Nitsch, Schwarzkogler: Writings of the Vienna Actionists*, Arkhive Seven, Atlas Press, 1999, p. 256.

4. Hollis Frampton, *Circles of Confusion: Film, Photography, Video, Texts 1968– 1980*, New York, Visual Studies Workshop Press, 1983, p. 26.

5. Liz Kotz, 'Language Between Performance and Photography', *OCTOBER*, no. 111, Cambridge, MA, MIT Press, Winter 2005, pp. 3–21.

6. Hollis Frampton, transcript entitled *Hollis Frampton on Hollis Frampton* (from course at SUNY Buffalo, Special Topics: Film-makers, session on September 16th, 1977), pp. 3–4. See Bruce Jenkins and Susan Krane, *Hollis Frampton: Recollections/Recreations*, Albright-Knox Art Gallery, Buffalo, NY, Cambridge, MA and London, MIT Press, 1984, p. 111.

7. Compare, for example, the photographic quality applied to Beuys' objects and performances as published in Caroline Tisdall's *Joseph Beuys* (Thames and Hudson, 1979) with the *Esssential Joseph Beuys* (Thames and Hudson, 1994). One recognises how the character of the object changes in these two records. In the earlier publication including photographs by Ute Klophaus, the use of a shorter depth of field and the grainy black and white print seems closer to the overall aesthetics associated with Beuys' practice. In the second publication in some photographs the use of colour, increased depth of field, and sharpened focus all act to remove the work from the overall look of Beuys' practice.

8. In a conversation with the author in 2003.

9. In a conversation with the author in 2006.

10. See Liz Kotz, 'Language Between Performance and Photography', *OCTOBER*, no. 111, Winter 2005, pp. 3–21.

THE *MEAT JOY* PHOTOGRAPHERS

Carolee Schneemann and Alice Maude-Roxby

The diverse practice of artist Carolee Schneemann offers a good starting point from which to examine the influence of different recording styles and the changing status, through time, of the performance document as artefact. The following extracts are from a conversation with Schneemann at her archive in New Paltz, New York, in March 2006. We met to discuss the varying ways in which her work has been documented with photography, film, and video.

I have been interested by the trajectory of processes that trigger one representation into another within the making of Schneemann's works. From drawing to performance, from performance to photography, from photography to installation, and then later, in works like *Unexpectedly Research*, 1962–1992–where she selected and presented images from photographic documentation of her performances alongside photographs of cultural artefacts that explicitly share iconography or gesture–Schneemann found visual connections past the event of the performance: a visual history of her practice immersed in a wider history of image making.

CAROLEE SCHNEEMANN: *The history of my performance work relies on archives of photographic documentation. Paradoxically I activated 'perform- ance art' within origins emerging directly out of the dimensionality of painting–now encapsulated in the still photograph. I still think of myself in essence as a painter remarking that at this moment 'performance art' is so densely inhabited, it no longer offers a blind terrain–it belongs to another generation removed from visual viscerality–anything comes and goes: song and dance, narrative, gender issues, self-confession, explicit political motives, gymnastics, theatrical and video references …*

Eye Body: 36 Transformative Actions for Camera, 1963, is a series of photographs taken through collaboration with the artist Erro who recorded Schneemann in an environment she had made within her studio. The environment in and with which the naked Schneemann physically interacts for *Eye Body* included painting constructions, kinetic objects, collage materials, works in progress, and live garter snakes. I anticipated from looking at the 36 photographs that make up *Eye Body*, which seem remarkably composed and could be thought of as precedents for subsequent works to camera by artists like Cindy Sherman, that this collaboration had developed

Schneemann Studio, New Paltz, NY, 2006, photographs © Jennifer Kotter.

over time. I learned that the piece was in fact the work of one shoot taking place within an intense, short period of time.

CS: *When I first saw the contacts of the photographs Erro had made of* Eye Body, *I thought they were remarkable–we had achieved my intention. We then made initial 8 by 10 inch prints and I took them to some major museum curators whom I thought would respond to this integration of the live vital nude as a collage material within my painting constructions. To a man–they were all men–they assured me* Eye Body *was bullshit. I've quoted their remarks, 'If you want to paint go back to your studio.' 'Stop running around naked.' 'This is narcissistic exhibitionism.' There was no aesthetic context for* Eye Body, *just as there was no initial context for* Fuses *Bob Morris called this 'lag-time in the art world'–another six or seven years before art historians bring focus to seemingly unprecedented work.* Interior Scroll *came into critical discourse when Moira Roth printed its image on the cover of an issue of* Women Artists *in the later 1970s.*

ALICE MAUDE-ROXBY: Are there other pieces, like *Eye Body*, which were performed to camera?

CS: *I would say all of my works with an audience are potentially alert to the camera.*

AMR: You think of those with an audience as 'performance to camera' also?

CS: *I would say yes. Within the solo works, being blinded by a flash is a most positive interaction! In the pieces where I am working with projections I am in darkness, I don't see the audience. So when the flash goes off–it is vibrant, participatory–like some kind of lightning bugs, opening space within space. At that point I can tell, 'They've got it!' Absolutely the right moment! At the back of my reptilian brain I know that is the moment I needed them to capture: an energy communication.*

Seen in the archive within the collective documentation for individual performances of Schneemann's work I was struck by the varied representations different photographers made of a single performance, and how the characteristics of each different photographic style seemed to bring out a different dimensionality to the content of the work. This is most dramatically seen in the multiple versions of *Interior Scroll* documented by Anthony McCall and Sally Dixon. Whilst these two documentations were made at different presentations of *Interior Scroll* made in 1975 and 1977, the gesture of Schneemann reading the scroll as she extracts it from her vagina, is seen more dynamically in one set of photographs. The gesture feels much more confrontational. As we discussed these photographs we also talked about the different contexts in which they had been published and the ways in which aspects of Schneemann's work have variously enabled and disabled the works' entrance into culture.

CS: *My mantra currently is that my early use of my naked body has obscured the full body of my work: installation, projection systems, electronics (starting in the 1960s with the complex multi-media of* Snows*).* Interior Scroll–The Cave *is consequential due to the unexpectedness, the overtness of the explicit body's actions, her speaking cunt, her double mouth. If I had construed the work as a theoretical text it would have been didactive, depictive.* Interior Scroll *is not simply transgressive physicality, a facing of the genital taboo but takes its power from a formal* visual *structure: the editing and phrasing, the interior rhythms of the visual material.*

The variations on the documentations of Interior Scroll *reflect the different temperaments of the individuals as much as their different sight lines. My selection from the documentation also has to do with rights: Anthony McCall was my husband in the 1970s and we collaborated on documenting each other's action events. He wasn't going to say, 'You have to pay me $150.00 or you can't use these negatives'.*

There are complexities and difficulties relating to the rights and copyrights of the photographic documentation of my work. In the 1960s no one had any money, I never paid anyone to photograph anything. When friends came with their cameras they were absolutely welcome; they could take whatever they wanted. The deal was, you can sell the photos but can I receive a contact print and have prints at cost? That was usually how it worked out. Since then, commercialisation and commodification have inflated expectations of the potential value of these images. A further complication: often I cannot afford the prices a photographer charges for use of my own imagery if I do not own the negative. It is important to note that academic presses expect free use of photographic material, or at best they offer a paltry usage fee.

As we looked through the archive of photographs of *Interior Scroll* I was surprised to see the small initiatory drawing that had been the starting

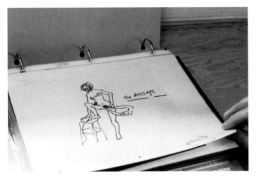

Schneemann Studio, New Paltz, N.Y., 2006, photograph © Jennifer Kotter.
Carolee Schneemann, Meat Joy, 1964, photograph by Manfred Schroeder.

point for the work. Relating to the process of drawings as precedents for performance, Schneemann wrote in her book *More than Meat Joy*:

> *Meat Joy* developed from dream sensation images gathered in journals. By February 1964 more elaborate drawings and notes accumulated as scraps of paper, on the wall over my bed, in tablets. I'd been concentrating on the possibility of capturing interactions between physical/metabolic changes, dream content, and my sensory orientation upon and after waking .... The drawings of movement, and notations on relations of colour, light, sound, language fragments, demanded organization, enaction and that I be able to sustain the connection to this imagery for an extended time–through the search for space, performers, funds, through painstaking rehearsals and the complexities of production down to the smallest details–all to achieve a fluid unpredictable performance.[1]

At least twelve different photographers documented *Meat Joy* at Judson Memorial Church in 1964. *Meat Joy* is described by Schneemann as having the character of 'an erotic rite: excessive, indulgent; a celebration of flesh'.[2] The piece had set parameters incorporating control in certain aspects, and improvisation in others. Within rehearsal for a segment of action referred to as 'The Paint Attack' the participants were given brushes and dry sponges to practice 'throwing and catching, drawing, falling, slapping, exchanging, stroking. Tenderly, then wildly.'[3] For the public performance these brushes and sponges were replaced with real paint, and also chickens, fish, and hot dogs.

cs: *What I find extraordinary is that in the case of* Meat Joy *there are photographs taken of almost exactly the same movement configurations by Tony Ray-Jones, Peter Moore, Al Giese, Robert McElroy. They have captured the same moment but their photographs are completely different: camera eye, position, exposure, focal length, film stock. That is their art. It is quite mysterious. I learn so much from the photographs with which my drawings form image history. The ones I most cherish are photographs replicating my initial drawings. Drawings made within the synaesthesia of consciousness/*

unconsciousness; kinaesthetic drawings, which predict or anticipate
photographed live action of the same image—big magic!

Footnotes

1. Carolee Schneemann *More than Meat Joy: Performance Works and Selected Writings*, 1979, Documentext, p. 63.
2. Carolee Schneemann, *Imaging Her Erotics, Essays, Interviews, Projects*, 2002. MIT Press, p. 61.
3. Carolee Schneemann, *More Than Meat Joy: Performance Works and Selected Writings*, 1979, Documentext, p. 78.
4. From a conversation with the author, April 2006.

From the *Meat Joy* Photographers' Archives

The group of twelve photographers who recorded *Meat Joy* in 1964 included professional photographers, artists, and friends. They were Arman, Peter Moore, Robert R. McElroy, Tony Ray-Jones, Dr. Manfred Schroeder, Harvey Zucker, Al Giese, Massal, Cheney, Fred W. McDarrah, Charles Rotenberg, and Harold Chapman. I visited the archives of some of these photographers and also looked at how their individual photographic versions of *Meat Joy* had been published within very different contexts.

Page 20–22

Carolee Schneemann, Meat Joy, 1964, photograph by Arman.
Carolee Schneemann, Meat Joy, 1964, photograph by Al Giese.
Carolee Schneemann, Meat Joy, 1964, photograph by Robert R.McElroy.
Claes Oldenburg, Ironworks/Fotodeath, 1961 photograph by Robert R.McElroy.

Robert R. McElroy recorded Happenings by Allan Kaprow, Claes Oldenburg, Jim Dine, and Robert Whitman from late 1950s to the 1960s. These photographs were published in Michael Kirby, *Happenings. An Illustrated Anthology*, E. P. Dutton Inc., New York, 1965. The early photographs are part of a wider record of the New York arts scene and included photographs of artists working and installing exhibitions, and of exhibition openings. Subsequently Robert R. McElroy worked for *Newsweek*. Within his archive are seen boxes of slides relating to early New York Happenings alongside photographs of editorial assignments for *Newsweek*—from Nixon to the Beatles.

Page 23

Carolee Schneemann, Meat Joy, 1964, photograph by Tony Ray-Jones.
Douglas, Isle of Wight, 1968, photograph by Tony Ray-Jones.

Tony Ray-Jones (1941–1972) photographed *Meat Joy*, 1964 whilst living in New York from 1961 to '66. Ray-Jones is probably best known for the

Carolee Schneemann, Meat Joy, 1964, photograph by Harvey Zucker.

body of work he made on his return to the UK – an extensive study of the English at leisure or on holiday, images of which are compiled in the book *A Day Off: An English Journal* (Thames & Hudson), published posthumously in 1975. Ray-Jones's photographs of early performances by Carolee Schneemann, Charlotte Moorman, and Schoenberg are held as part of his archive at the National Media Museum in Bradford.

Pages 24–25
Carolee Schneemann's Meat Joy, 1964, photograph by Fred W.McDarrah.
Paradise Now by the Living Theatre at the Brooklyn Academy of Music, October 14th 1968, Fred W.McDarrah.
A drag queen beauty pageant at Town Hall, February 20th 1967, photograph by Fred W.McDarrah.
Susan Sontag in a draft protest gets arrested at the Whitehall Street Army Recruiting Center, December 5th 1967, photograph by Fred W.McDarrah.
Grace Paley leads a march against the war, March 19th 1969, photograph by Fred W.McDarrah.
Wallace, Humphrey, Nixon subject of Yayoi Kusama's election day performance in front of Board of Elections, November 3rd 1968, photograph by Fred W.McDarrah.

Fred W. McDarrah's photograph of *Meat Joy*, 1964 is published in the book *Anarchy, Protest and Rebellion: And the Counterculture That Changed America*, Thunder's Mouth Press, 2003, authored with Gloria S.

See photograph captions on page 18.

All photographs by Tony Ray-Jones are © NMPFT-Tony Ray-Jones/Science & Society Picture Library.
See photograph captions on page 18.

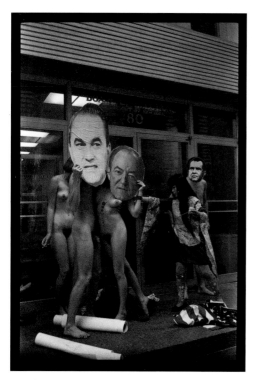

See photograph captions on page 18.

See photograph captions on page 18.

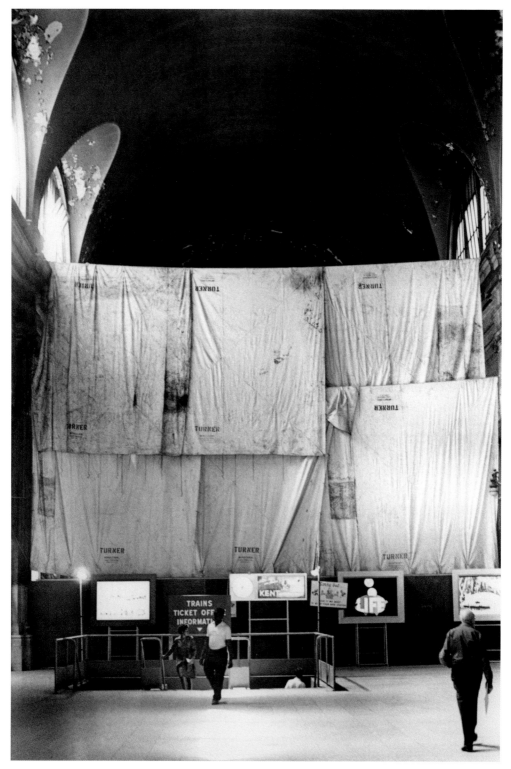

McDarrah and Timothy McDarrah. In this book McDarrah's photograph of *Meat Joy* is published alongside images of public demonstrations and protest. This visual context acts to draw out the very radical nature of Schneemann's work. Other photographic publications by the McDarrahs include *Gay Pride: Photographs from Stonewall to Today*, A Cappella Books, 1994; *Kerouac and Friends: A Beat Generation Album*, Thunder's Mouth Press, 1985; and *Greenwich Village*, Corinth Books, 1963.

Page 26–27
The Destruction of Penn Station 22nd August 1963, photograph by Peter Moore.
Carolee Schneemann, Meat Joy, 1964, photograph by Peter Moore.

The most expansive performance photography archive I visited was that of Peter Moore (1932–1993). The archive included approximately 300,000 photographs of avant-garde works dedicated to the recording of ephemeral events. It was interesting to see Moore's performance photographs in relation to examples of his independent practice. Published in his book, *The Destruction of Penn Station* (D.A.P., 2000) are photographs Moore took consistently through three years of the gradual destruction of Penn Station from 1963 to 1966. In Moore's photographs of the demolition of Penn Station the gradual disappearance of the station is recorded as an on-going event. As in his performance photographs there is the same attention to the presence of the public, their utilisation of the building, and the changing light and space as the station becomes increasingly clad in tarpaulins.

GUTAI AND PHOTOGRAPHY

Shimamoto Shozo and Alice Maude-Roxby
November 2005

Gutai group was formed under the leadership of artist Yoshihara Jiro in 1954, in the Kansai region of Japan. Artists included Shiraga Kazuo, Shimamoto Shozo, Kanayma Akira, Murakami Saburo, Tanaka Atsuko, and others. Gutai can be translated as 'embodiment'. In Gutai works, this term is characterised as the sensuous and physical impact of action onto materials. Mud, water, and paint, for example, were intensely activated through actions of kicking, striking, or being blasted through cannons.

From 1955, the artists self-published the Gutai journal to circulate their work. In the 1950s Japanese critical arts press, Gutai was considered both provincial and frivolous in contrast to Tokyo-based artists whose representational work, a surrealist based social realism, was considered intellectual and political. Sending out the Gutai journal, the group made direct allegiances with artists involved in radical developments in painting and sculpture in the USA and Europe. This included artists in European L'art Informel, COBRA, and abstract expressionism, as well as artists engaged in time-based actions and Happenings in the USA.

The Gutai group disbanded in 1970 when Yoshihara Jiro died.

ALICE MAUDE-ROXBY: Could you tell me about Gutai's background and how the artists came to site specific performances?

SHIMAMOTO SHOZO: I had known Yoshihara, who founded Gutai, since 1947 or '48. Yoshihara did not wish to have 'disciples', it wasn't in his character, but I was the first one who managed to join him. This was the beginning of the first group. In time there were about seven members. But they all gave up! Yoshihara was very severe, he had very strict rules and I was the only one who remained. I found ten new members for the group, but again they all gave up. Yoshihara was so sad that he wanted to give up too. Then I made a proposal: let's do something new, let's find another place for our performances, somewhere in Ashiya, an open air space. This attracted interest from new members and in this way Yoshihara founded Gutai.

AMR: I'm curious about the current interest in, and status of, the photographic documentation of Gutai actions as artefacts in Japan.

SS: I think the photographs of Gutai actions are really important, but this is a personal opinion. In Japan these photographs are not really considered, there is little interest in them. In my thinking the important aspect of the photographs is that they mark the time of this work, they prove how early these pieces were made. But in general in Japan the most

Shimamoto Shozo, 1956, photograph by Ohtsuji Kiyoji. See full contact print on page 26
Photographs by Ohtsuji Kiyoji © Ohtsuji Seiko.

important value relating to this work is that the photograph must be technically 'good', the importance is attached to this quality rather than to the photograph's content.

When I made those pieces the most important thing was the work: the performance itself. I was interested in being there, in that moment: being a person who experiences the sensation of the work through all of his body. Not just to see, or to hear, but to sense through all of the body. The photographs are important because they remind one of the performance but don't show everything. After the event the photographs were important but at the time I really wasn't thinking about that at all, I was only thinking about the lived experience. Later we understood that the photographs are important, as a 'witness' to the events.

Now the films and photographs are very precious to me because they also document the history of Gutai. They act as witness to the actions and also to how Yoshihara founded Gutai and to my own involvement

within that group and that time. The films and photographs are a kind of treasure.

When we made the work I realised the photographs could be important as a way of circulating our ideas: I printed some of this material and tried to spread it in the world. Unfortunately within Japan I had no reply, they were quite cold to the material. I found more interest abroad.

AMR. Do you mean through the journal? I read that Gutai group produced the first issue by hand in a shed with a printing press, can you tell me about that?

SS: Yes, I printed it by hand, here in the shed next door. I set all the characters by hand, one by one. At the time I didn't know anything about mail art, but I had the idea that we should make a journal and send it out. Within Japan we had almost no response. In the group there were mixed feelings about this handmade publication. Yoshihara said it was very good and I was a genius, but some members thought it wasn't any good, as it wasn't 'professional'. Yoshihara said 'Let's try it anyway, we'll send it out and see what happens'. There was no way other than to do it by ourselves.

The Gutai journal became famous when Jackson Pollock died and some issues were found in his studio. A representative for Pollock got in touch with us. That was how the Gutai group became well known.

AMR: It is interesting how effective sending the journal was in terms of establishing connections to artists in the United States and Europe. In one issue you published the correspondence with Pollock's estate, showing the connection between Gutai and radical movements in painting in the States which, as I understand, you had been unaware of until then. But I thought Allan Kaprow also connected aspects of Gutai works to Happenings and the curator Tapié was acknowledging the work of Gutai in relation to developments in painting occuring at that time in France.

SS: Tapié was interested in selling the work. He didn't like my hole pieces, he considered them to be dirty work or something which was not really work at all. He told me, 'Don't make this sort of work anymore'. I wasn't really aware of Kaprow's interest until much later. In 1998 I was invited to Taiwan by Kaprow, and had the chance to speak with him. At that point I realised Yoshihara had blocked a communication Kaprow tried to establish with us. Perhaps Yoshihara preferred the more conservative direction of Tapié who wanted to exhibit the Gutai paintings but was not interested in the actions.

AMR: I found the Super 8 films documenting Gutai very interesting. The films show a side to the work which is completely missing from the photographs. There is a humour in your work on film, for example, seeing the timing in *Please Walk on Here*, 1955, with the sudden gesture of stumbling as part of the piece. Comparing the films (which are silent) to the photographs I realised how much action is missing from this documentation: the sound, the explosions, the smashing of glass.

SS: Yes, that was all part of it. Humour was part of my work. But in Japan 'funny' is no good. You are good if you are serious. Within the group I was always declassed because of this. Other Gutai artists were careful to show serious expressions whilst making the work and being filmed or photographed. But I didn't care about that. I wanted to do something new without thinking about anything, without being limited. For me, in this kind of art, it is also important that there is a danger about it.

AMR: In the Ashiya archive I saw that the media recognised different potentials in photographing or filming Gutai: for example, at one event fashion models are photographed within the works. There is also documentation of assignments from the BBC and *LIFE* magazine. Some amazing photographs show *LIFE* correspondents documenting Gutai in 1956. Can you tell me about this?

SS: Yoshihara contacted *LIFE* to make a report about Gutai performances. He told all Gutai members not to take photographs because only *LIFE* would record the event but the article was never published. This was difficult because we have absolutely no documentation of the work: I know someone took photos of the cannon I made but I have never seen them. I don't know why they didn't publish these photographs but there is no other record of the event. Even now I would like to get those pictures.

Translation by Andrea Mardegan.

Contact print. The 2nd Gutai Art Exhibition featuring works by Shimamoto Shozo, Murakami Saburo, Tanaka Atsuko and Shiraga Kazuo, 1956. Photographs by Ohtsuji Kiyoji © Ohtsuji Seiko.

NOTE OF PHOTOGRAPHY

Ohtsuji Kiyoji

Photographer Ohtsuji Kiyoji (1923–2001) documented actions by Shimamoto Shozo, Murakami Saburo, Tanaka Atsuko, and Shiraga Kazuo at the 2nd Gutai Art Exhibition in October 1956. Gutai actions were also photographed extensively by the artists themselves and these photographs, generally anonymously credited, are held in the Ashiya City Museum of Art and History. In his own practice as a photographer Ohtsuji worked with performance to camera, photographs of objects and street photography. He also extensively documented art events in museums. Ohtsuji was a key member of the avant garde in Japan, he co-founded Experimental Workshop (a radical cross-disciplinary artists' group) and wrote articles on photography. The following extracts come from his book, Note of Photography, *Bijutsu-Shuppansha, May 1989.*

from 'Photographs [I] want to take'[1]

I could reference several works of art that reflect what I describe as the transcendence of reality, or the discovery of an alternative reality. Duchamp's objects, for instance, would be paradigmatic of such a position. *Urinal* (Marcel Duchamp's *Fountain*, 1917), is often cited as a seminal work of art, but honestly, I never really understood it in the past. I thought it was a kind of cheap pun. However, as time went by, I began to realise that a different world unfolds behind the banality of it. I was seized by the desire to be able to move freely between the reality of the mundane urinal to the reality of a urinal in another dimension. That was the beginning. The problem is not in the method of expression. If the method of expression had anything to do with it, it would only become an issue once I learned to move freely between the concept of different realities.

It will not become relevant until I begin to consider how to translate a concept, which can only be captured in my head, into a visual form in everyday reality. Although the title implies another reality behind the mundane reality, I have never seen a photograph of Duchamp's urinal that visually transcends the expression of an ordinary urinal. In Duchamp's case, this is probably to be expected in the initial stages of such a proposition. However, as a photographer, my desire is to make this conceptual shift using the medium of photography. I do not want it simply to shift in any old direction. I want to photograph a thing to shift in the very particular direction that I perceive it, and in such a way that any observer can perceive it in this way, regardless of my own subjective sentiments. I do not yet know whether or not such a thing is possible. Nevertheless, one thing is certain. This challenge is central to my desire to confront the medium of photography.

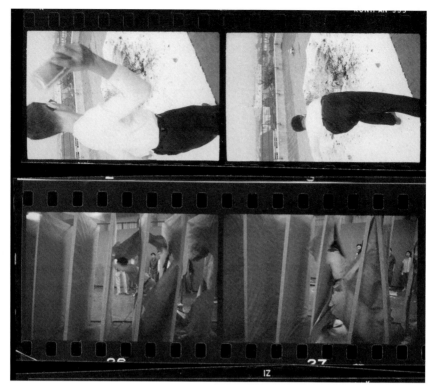

Shimamoto Shozo, 1956 and *Murakami Saburo's Passage*, 1956, photographs by Ohtsuji Kiyoji. See full contact print on page 26.

(opposite) *Portrait of the Artist–in Nobuya Abe's Atelier*, 1950, photograph by Ohtsuji Kiyoji. Photographs by Ohtsuji Kiyoji © Ohtsuji Seiko.

From 'Assignments for Beginners'[2]

By space-time, I am referring to the 'space-time continuum', which is a familiar term from Einstein's Theory of Special Relativity and science fiction novels. It is very familiar to us in terms of the relativity of time and space in photography. In other words, effects such as camera shake, blurring through movement of subject, and long exposures, as well as snapshot photography, show this. Multiple exposures and sandwiching multiple negatives, as well as the technique known as fixed frame long exposure, are also instances of space-time in photography.

One might go so far as to say that no photograph is unrelated to the space-time effect. Even with an ordinarily photographed picture, if you look at it intently, the eternally still scene starts to appear increasingly strange. One cannot help but feel that this is a different sight than that which we normally experience. This is even more true with blurred photographs and multiple exposure photos, which are markedly unreal. This makes us realise that photography is, without a doubt, a device that highlights relationships between space and time. Photography is commonly thought of as something that provides a true representation of reality. In most cases, this is not so far from the truth.

Translation by Takako Jin

Footnotes

1. Ohtsuji Kiyoji, 'Note of Photography', *Bijutsu-Shuppansha*, May 1989, pp. 193–198.
2. Ohtsuji Kiyoji, 'Note of Photography', *Bijutsu-Shuppansha*, May 1989, pp. 79–84.

BEHOLD!

Kathy O'Dell

Perhaps it is not surprising that one of the earliest words, etymologically, to be used as a command to look at something–'Behold!'–contains within it the command to touch.[1] Moreover, not only is haptic experience invoked in this command, but existence itself–Be!

A mere play on words? Perhaps, but the combination of meanings is worth pondering, and *Live Art on Camera* encourages the viewer to do so. The exhibition emphasises the role of the photographer in recording live art events. The photographer's physical presence at these events is without question (he or she had to 'be' there), as is the photographer's handling of the medium (he or she had to 'hold' the camera, touch the shutter release, and manipulate the film). Subsequently, the photographers, as well as the visitors to the exhibition and the viewers of its parts reproduced in this catalogue, have the opportunity to behold the resulting photographic prints and to question what the images and the processes through which they were created mean. The situation is similar when it comes to the filmmaker or videographer of live art events and their viewers.

To these connotations of the term 'behold', another can be added: the connotation of ownership, as in being 'beholden' to someone or some-thing. This more abstract, transitive meaning is defined in the *Oxford English Dictionary* as follows: 'to hold by some tie of duty or obligation, to retain as a client or person in duty bound'.[2] Minding this connotation as we look at the works in this exhibition brings the art market to our considerations, in a more substantive way than the mere recognition that all works of art are born into the world of commerce whether their makers wish this or not. This transitive meaning, when added to the others, raises questions of power: Who is in charge when we look at these photographs? Where does the obligation of interpretation lie? To whom are we, as viewers, bound by our interpretations? To the individuals pictured? To the photographer, filmmaker, or videographer who made the photograph, film, or video to look the way it does? To art history? To ourselves? To the social context in which the images were made or to that in which they now appear?

In this essay, I should like to explore the dynamics that come into play when we as viewers of recorded live art events respond to the tacit, in-ternalised command 'Behold!' and are attentive to its multiple meanings. Examining what it is to see, to touch, to be, and to own, and questioning how those experiences play out, into, and around each other as we observe a selection of photographs in the *Live Art on Camera* exhibition and catalogue may yield important information about the viewing of recorded images of live action in general.

Behold: Four women on a park bench in unconventional positions, lying on their left hips, legs sticking up and resting against the back of the bench, heads hanging off the seat, one woman's hair touching the ground, one woman balancing herself by planting the top of her head and the palm of her right hand squarely on the sidewalk, another woman balanced by pressing her left forearm onto the ground. Bodies akimbo, in stark contrast to the more conventional position of audience members, who may have assembled by happenstance, having interrupted their walks through the park (one woman pushes a pram) to observe what they may or may not have recognised as a performance by avant-garde choreographer Trisha Brown. This black and white image, taken by photographer Babette Mangolte, appeared as a full-page photograph on the left side of a layout in the magazine *Art and Artists* in January 1974. The photograph functioned as a record of Brown's *Group Accumulation*, performed in New York City's Central Park in 1973.[3] On the right side of the layout, opposite the photograph, is the opening section of 'Moving Structures', an interview with several artists, including Brown.

While the performance looks compelling (and no doubt was, knowing Brown's work), what is of more interest to me for the moment is the position of the audience relative to my own, which I share with the photographer, at least in terms of point of view. I am confronted with a line of curiously perched dancers, extending from the foreground to just beyond the middle ground of the image, as well as with a line of a dozen or more audience members, most of whom appear to be watching the dancers, but may have been stealing a glance at the photographer (and now, in a sense, at me, as well). What I do not see is whether there were more audience members to Mangolte's (my) right. Might there have been a semicircle of viewers swinging out to the right from my point of view, beyond the edge of the picture, then curving back in toward the bench? Am I therefore seeing only a portion of the semicircle? As it is, the line of audience members starts at the far end of the park bench and extends at about a 45-degree angle to the middle of the right-hand side of the photograph. Were there viewers behind the park bench who have been cropped from the photograph, as well? Only the photographer knows for sure, but whatever the factual answers, the photographic record provides today's viewer a subtly strategic entrée into a field of questions having to do with seeing, being, touching, and owning.

This subtle strategy is realised in a formal sense by the very cropping that Mangolte (or perhaps the photoeditor at *Art and Artists*, or perhaps the two of them together) carried out. That which lies within the confines of the photograph, specifically between the line of dancers at the left and the line of audience members extending from it, creates an upside-down V-shape section of sidewalk–a path which cannot be visually travelled very far without being thwarted by either the line of audience members or dancers. Rather, after taking in these pictured individuals, one's gaze seems forced to retreat along the path back down toward the photographer's own feet and, more significantly, off to the right. As one's gaze moves to the right, one moves directly and strategically ('strategic' on the photographer's and/or photoeditor's parts) into the printed interview.

Once again, as interested as I might be in the questions and answers posed in the 'Moving Structures' interviews, the questions listed above –about the dynamics of seeing and the ways in which they intertwine with the dynamics of touching, being, and owning–are more compelling to me here. Starting with the haptic, it is important to note that far more people would come to know Mangolte's photograph in and after 1974 by holding the actual magazine in their hands than by looking at the discrete photograph framed and mounted on the wall of a gallery. The haptic experience one has when viewing images published in print is an experience that works in provocatively duplicative ways to tie viewer, photographer, performers, and, in this case, their audience, together across time. For the viewer handles the magazine and touches the photograph in the here and now, just as Mangolte handled the camera and touched its shutter release back in 1973, just as the two dancers touched the ground to balance themselves, just as the man in the distance touches the inside of his pocket,

Trisha Brown's *Group Accumulation*, photograph © Babette Mangolte as it appeared in *Art & Artists* in January 1974.

and the woman touches the handle of the pram, and so forth.

However unconsciously one might experience this string of events unwinding from the present into the past and back again, the winding binds
the viewer, however conceptually and philosophically, to the photographer
and to those whom she or he photographed. This tie hinges on choice, past
and present. Choices have been and still are being made–to perch on the
park bench, to stop and watch, to depress the camera shutter, to behold the
photograph now. The unwinding and rewinding of time and experience
–a winding that is not as often parallelled, in today's digital age, in material terms by the winding of actual film around a spool inside the camera
(but is still embedded in our cognitive makeup for the following to be
true)–binds those choices and the individuals who make them together
in a type of agreement that is contract-like, as I have written elsewhere.[4]
Another way of thinking of the complex notion of the contract is to say
that the viewer of a photograph in the here and now not only beholds
but is also beholden to what he or she views and to those involved in its
making and recording.

This sense of being beholden to, or responsible for, is perhaps most
obvious in photographs of performances that involve risk and, more to
the point, botched risk. For wherever risk is involved, the question arises
whether the person taking the risk is thoroughly capable of taking responsibility for him or herself. A photograph from U.S. artist Chris Burden's
infamous 1971 performance *Shoot* makes this point. Burden arranged to
have a sharpshooter friend graze his arm when firing at him with a 22-
calibre rifle. The artist, sharpshooter, photographer Alfred Lutjeans, and
the few friends whom Burden invited to the event all knew what was to
occur (were 'bound' so to speak, in an agreement to let the event occur).
Not all went as planned, however. Either the sharpshooter, or Burden, or
both, became nervous and moved, and the bullet went much deeper than
planned. Lutjeans captured a moment, somewhere between the shooting
and the impact, in which both the sharpshooter and Burden are blurred,
and it is this photograph that has come to personify the performance.

The photograph I am more interested in is the less often seen image
of Burden sitting in a chair, glassy-eyed, staring straight at Lutjeans.
Someone (it is unclear whether it is a man or a woman, as we see only
hands) grasps Burden's arm with one hand, and with the other applies tape
to the bloodstained bandage covering the artist's wound. Lutjeans
manages to pull together in one image all four issues at stake in the act of
beholding. As Burden returns our gaze, he binds us, as he did his friends
and Lutjeans, into his act of self-directed violence. In addition to empha-
sising the act of seeing, the photograph highlights touching, as the disem-
bodiment of the nursing hands makes the administering of touch
a focal point. Concepts of being also come to mind, inasmuch as
being–life itself–was pushed to the limit here. Finally, issues of owning
arise as we ask where responsibility lies in a performance such as this.
Who 'owned' the right to stop the performance, to allow it to continue, or

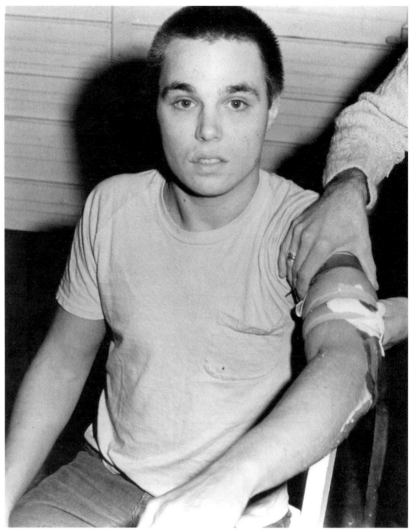

CHRIS BURDEN
Shoot
November 19, 1971
#5

Chris Burden, *Shoot*, 1971 © Chris Burden. Courtesy Gagosian Gallery.

to attend to its aftermath? More to the point, who owns the myriad violent events, self-inflicted or otherwise, that occur every day, for which this performance serves as a metaphor? Staring at the photographer as Burden did in this photograph makes clear the photographer's (and our own) presence at the event and responsibility in and for it (or those for which it stands as metaphor). Burden's *Shoot* is the consummate 'limit-text', taking questions of seeing, touching, being, and owning to the limit, laying them all out clearly, thus reminding us as viewers to be sure to ask them of ourselves as we view recorded events of any variety, up to and including these limits, on a daily basis.

Ironically, the photographer has been historically invisible in the contract-like agreement that pertains to the recording of live events, even though he or she may have been the most engaged in a material sense. Negotiating with the artist over how a series of photographs of a live art event would look, whether and how much the artist would pay for the photograph, and so forth, the photographer would often culminate these negotiations in some form of written agreement that could be considered contractual. Fortunately, this exhibition disallows such invisibility. Moreover, by drawing attention to the photographer, as curator Alice Maude-Roxby has so aptly done in *Live Art on Camera*, she also draws attention to you and to me, and to the fact of our sharing with the photographer his or her physical point of view, a point of view laced with seeing, touching, owning, and being. The works in the exhibition and catalogue trigger all these experiences to varying degrees.

Mangolte further mined the possibilities of the haptic in a collaboration with choreographer, dancer, and filmmaker Yvonne Rainer in the mid-1970s, in which they together produced a photographic work consisting of numerous photographs laid out on the pages of the art magazine *Interfunktionen*, number 12, 1975. Several photographs occupied each page, with lines of text appearing inside cartoon-type boxes, complete with arrows directing attention to the person supposedly saying the lines.[5] The piece encouraged touching by the inclusion of foldout pages with which the viewer was meant to interact. When viewers did so, they would see, for example, a series of photographs in which a woman appears to be walking away from the camera, ultimately joined by a man who follows her into the distance. The sequential, storyboard-like appearance of the photographs lends them a cinematic quality–not surprising, perhaps, considering the project's date, which harkens to the early years of Rainer's filmmaking and aligns with the very beginning of Mangolte's own career as a filmmaker.[6] The artists' collaboration on the *Interfunktionen* piece demonstrated the ability to share ownership of it, and its interactive composition allows us to share ownership of it, as well.

Mangolte's installation in the exhibition emphasises the haptic in similarly obvious, but also surprising ways. On a long table are displayed scores of photographs the viewer is invited to leaf through, very obviously engaging them in a haptic experience, while on the wall are mounted photographs which one may only view from a distance. A banister has been installed to assure such distance, which disallows touching. Surprisingly, the absence of the possibility of touching only seems to accentuate its importance. This irony brings to mind the irony inherent in philosopher Martin Heidegger's early twentieth-century theorisations of being (*Dasein*) in which, interestingly, he invoked the haptic, coining the terms 'present-at-hand' (*vorhanden*) and 'ready-to-hand' (*zuhanden*). In his seminal 1927 book *Being and Time* (*Sein und Zeit*),[7] he uses the term 'present-at-hand' to describe those things right in front of us that we consciously pay attention to, while 'ready-to-hand' might encompass those very same things but, given our active involvement with or use of them,

Yvonne Rainer, *Kristina (For a ...Opera)*, Photos by Babette Mangolte, arranged on the pages with the assistance of Benjamin H.D. Buchloh, *Interfunktionen* No 12, 1975, pp. 13–47 © Babette Mangolte and Yvonne Rainer

those things seemingly fade away into the activities in which we engage them.[8] The irony here is that for the 'present-at-hand' to exist, the 'ready-to-hand' has to have already existed or, I would argue, to exist simultaneously. Rather than being separate experiences, in other words, they are codependent. Viewing Mangolte's photographs from a distance, their 'present-at-hand-ness' can only be fully informed by viewers engaging in the 'ready-to-hand-ness' of those on the table, and vice versa.

The inclusion in the exhibition of photographs that a team of *LIFE* magazine photographers took in 1956 of a performance by Japanese artist Shiraga Kazuo, who belonged to the avant-garde Gutai Theater, brings the full complement of issues I have been discussing to bear. The performance took place on a beach and entailed Shiraga standing inside an open cone-shaped structure made of about one dozen thick wooden poles, each approximately five metres tall, the bottoms of which had been placed in the sand to form a circle about one human body length in diameter, and the tops of which were brought together to form a point. The tops of the poles rested against each other in precarious balance. To the right of the structure in one photograph stands another structure, this one composed of a wooden ladder almost the same height, around which stand numerous men in suits or raincoats and on which stands a photographer taking a photograph of Shiraga. Dressed in dark pants and shirtless, the artist is swinging an axe, bringing it dangerously close to the poles. One assumes from the photograph that Shiraga intended to keep swinging until the poles fell, putting himself (and perhaps the photographers around the ladder) at risk.

The article was never published in *LIFE*, but the Gutai Theater published the photograph in their own magazine, and Allan Kaprow published it in his groundbreaking and widely distributed book *Assemblage, Environments & Happenings* in 1965.[9] Arguably, the photo-

Reporters from the American LIFE magazine photographing Shiraga Kazuo participating in the "One-Day-Only Outdoor Exhibition (Ruins Exhibition)" at the Yoshihara Oil Mill Nishinomiya Refinery, April 1956. Photographer unknown. ©: The former members of the Gutai Art Association. Courtesy: Ashiya City Museum of Art & History.

graph could be seen as a table of contents for an entire generation of artists and photographers engaged in live art.

Seeing and touching are underscored in the photograph by the multiple lines of vision and points of view–more than usual for a photograph of a live event. For what is really being photographed here is not the performance *per se*, but the photographers who are photographing the event. The photographer, whose position we share, cared deeply about creating a formally satisfying composition, and indeed it is, in all its symmetry. The photograph we are looking at, then, is itself about the very act of seeing and touching; it is about the photographer whose position we share seeing the photographer on the ladder and touching the camera release just as the other photographer touched his. Shiraga's risk-taking also brings issues of the haptic to the fore, along with issues of being, as he risked the collapse of heavy timber onto his unprotected body. And finally, the issue of ownership arises in *LIFE* magazine's having blocked any other photographers from recording Shiraga's performance. The magazine wished to retain ownership. Fortunately, the Gutai Theater managed to publish this photograph, and Kaprow managed to publish it once again, ushering it into the annals of art history as perhaps the most consummate example of 'live art on camera' and the complex issues such recorded imagery raises.

Other examples of still photography, as well as video and film, on exhibit in *Live Art on Camera*, await our interactions with them as beholders. As you explore these examples, allow them to engage you in a questioning of the fullest meaning of what it is to behold. What we discover in this process can lead us to observe the recordings of everyday life, for which live art serves as a metaphor, in a deeper, more responsive, and more responsible manner.

Footnotes

1. The *Oxford English Dictionary* dates the first recorded use of the term 'behold' to 971 A.D. See http://dictionary.oed.com/cgi/entry/50019713?query_type=word& queryword=behold&first=1&max_to_show=10&sort_type=alpha&result_place=1. Accessed June 2007.

2. 'Beholden' *Oxford English Dictionary*, http://dictionary.oed.com/cgi/ entry/5001976?query_type=word=behold&first=1&max_to_show=10&sort_ type=alpha&result_place=1. Accessed June 2007.

3. Effie Stephano, 'Moving Structures', *Art and Artists*, vol. 8, no. 10, issue 94, January 1974, pp. 16–21.

4. See Kathy O'Dell, *Contract with Skin: Masochism, Performance Art, and the 1970s*, Minneapolis, University of Minnesota Press, 1998.

5. Yvonne Rainer, *Kristina (For a ... Opera)*, photos by Babette Mangolte, arranged on the pages with the assistance of Benjamin H.D. Buchloh, *Interfunktionen*, no. 12, 1975, pp. 13–47.

6. Yvonne Rainer completed her first film, *Volleyball (Foot Film)*, in 1967. Babette Mangolte completed her first film, *What Maisie Knew*, in 1975.

7. Martin Heidegger, *Sein und Zeit*, Halle, Max Niemeyer Verlag, 1927; first translated into English as *Being and Time*, trans. John Macquarrie and Edward Robinson, New York, Harper, 1962.

8. For a contemporary view of these Heideggerian notions, see Paul Dourish, *Where the Action Is: The Foundations of Embodied Interaction*, Cambridge, MA, MIT Press, 2001.

9. Allan Kaprow, *Assemblage, Environments & Happenings*, New York, Harry N. Abrams, 1965.

FIVE RECORDS

Leda Papaconstantinou and Alice Maude-Roxby
May 2007

ALICE MAUDE-ROXBY: I'm interested in Roy Tunnicliffe's photographs of your early works, in particular the performance *Deaf and Dumb*. The photograph looks like a portrait, was this piece performance to camera?

LEDA PAPACONSTANTINOU: I chose to work with my friend Roy Tunnicliffe, who was a painter and photographer, working mostly in black and white. His paintings were photorealist and the images had a strong surrealist feeling. He was the first to record my performances, but only my earliest pieces. He committed suicide in the early 1970s. *Deaf and Dumb* was a durational piece that I repeated for over a week in several different locations in London and Maidstone. In order to understand the work, one has to consider its specific time and place. In 1971, there were major differences between Greek and British culture regarding physicality. In Britain there seemed to be a complete lack of physicality. Greece, on the other hand, was entirely physical. Since then a lot has changed: physical exchange in Britain has now become, almost, a social must.

I walked about with drawings over my eyes, waiting to see how people would react. In general people responded as if I were deaf but not blind. They would not look me in the eye, that this contact was not part of their culture was the first point I attacked. Roy spent a lot of time with me while I was making that piece. He didn't take any photographs, he just watched. After a week he asked to make the portrait of me with those eyes. He also made a brilliant photograph of me wearing very dark sunglasses. He liked the idea of a portrait where one cannot see the eyes, where eye contact is denied.

AMR: It is interesting that so many very different photographers documented your work. Each seems to have applied a particular way of seeing. For example, can you speak about the documentation made by Erricos Meliones of your piece *The Box*?

LP: Erricos Meliones is a fashion photographer. *The Box* was my first performance piece in a gallery. The gallery wanted 'a good photographer' and hired Meliones. He was very interested in the performance but found it really difficult that we were not posing for the camera. We were performing and he had to follow us, something he was not used to at all. He began by asking us to freeze for the camera, but Lesley and I refused, so he just had to go along with it. I was not happy with his photographs at the time. They were so removed from my idea of what it means to record work. They were too glossy, too pretty. The actuality of the piece was quite different from what the pictures show. It was much messier in reality; it was quite grotesque and not at all glamorous. We lived for hours each day in those small spaces, 1.5 cubic metres. It was hot and smelt bad. The photographer chose angles carefully in order to cut all that mess out. His viewpoint, since he actually came into the space, was entirely different

from that of the audience. The audience viewed the piece through lenses placed on thin card-board walls. Viewing the piece through a lens made the spectator feel very distant when,
in fact, they were very close to us. They spoke very loudly; it took a lot of effort and control not to respond to the comments. I think Meliones was totally overwhelmed by what he saw and his response was to try to glamorise the grotesque.

AMR: It's interesting to compare these to images like Alexis Stamatiadis' photographs of *Dim Landscapes*.

LP: Alexis Stamatiadis was not a professional photographer. He made architectural drawings as a career. But he was a total photography maniac: taking photographs, developing, printing. He recorded all of my work until he divorced my best friend. Then he stopped.

Alexis took brilliant photographs. With *Dim Landscapes*, he photographed through the transparent polythene that hung freely in a structure made of plastic sacking. It looked like a uterus; we had sprayed the plastic red. The photographs seem incredibly true to the piece, absolutely representing how it was. When I look at them now I think I must have directed him but in fact he was just there, independently shooting away. Alexis felt a part of the performance, and you can see this in the documentation. How he was different from the fashion photographer who visited the piece three or four times to get shots is very obvious. Alexis' photographs are on the spot, true to space and time.

People don't work like this anymore, performance has changed. Attitudes are different: now performance is very staged, and on top of that the photographs are also staged. The artwork can, in reality, be 'nothing' but the documentation may act as a post mortem script for the performance. My approach has always been completely different: I allow the photographer no time to make notes, I need them to take photographs which are absolutely close to the feeling of the pieces, so that I can learn about my work from their documentation. That material is the mirror of my particular time in space. For me a true and accurate depiction of the real time and space of a performance reflects my feeling of scale and relation to the world. That is very important to the work itself. I won't change; but it's ok for younger artists to do things differently.

AMR: The photographs of *Bouboulitsa's Dream* are much more classical. They make me think of travelling studio shots: a set of images with individual character portraits, acting as a visual lexicon of the piece's components. They are quite unusual as performance photographs.

LP: Well, I'm pleased if you see it like that. Dimitris Papadimas was a completely different kind of photographer, one who loved to work with people. He was a documentary photographer who always carried a camera. He was born in Alexandria and was introduced to photography by an Englishman who looked after him and encouraged him in photography. He took photographs for museums, for example, the Museum of Folk Art. I asked him to take these photos like individual portraits. We were trying to get local people involved in the performance as much as possible. I wanted them each to have a photograph to keep, taken in a style that was both dignified and humorous.

AMR: Alongside your performances you also filmed yourself and made films of performers for works like *Oh Godard*, *Bite*, and *Votive*. Could you tell me about that transition and whether you were intentionally trying to record the body in a particular way? I notice that you close tight on the body. This

Leda Papaconstantinou, *Deaf and Dumb*, 1971, photograph by Roy Tunnicliffe.

Deaf And Dumb

I painted large eyes on my closed eyelids.

On a sign, placed below my breast the following statement was written:

I AM DEAF AND DUMB. PLEASE COMMUNICATE WITH ME IN OTHER WAYS.

Hardly anyone noticed that I was simply blind.

Leda Papaconstantinou

tight framing feels emphasised, for example, when the tattooed arm of the second figure cuts into the frame.

LP: The change from performance to film came about as 'the moving image' became a new thing in the art world. Performance was very loose and without definite boundaries. It could incorporate a lot. Working in film was feasible; there was no sense of specialisation at that time. Now specialisation has become incredibly important, but at that time there was a lot of borrowing across media. I never pretended I was a filmmaker or a sound artist, although I did a lot of sound recording too. To explain how I came to make *Oh Godard* is complicated. Godard was my hero but it was actually Eisenstein who was in my mind before him. The scream in *Battleship Potemkin* was the prime image that motivated me to make this film. I was shy about saying that the piece was an homage to Eisenstein. I felt closer to Godard and dedicated my portrait to him instead. The image context I worked with came from these two great personalities, and the piece was the shortest ritual I could think of. The work was totally controlled although I was filming myself. I had looked in a mirror and worked out the height through marks on a wall. I sat down and did it, looked at the result and it was exactly what I wanted.

I was excited that the material of film gave me a sense of permanence; it was also far more private and much more related to myself. In *Votive* I directed but didn't appear in the piece myself. I gave myself the chance to see one of my performances and 'take it down' so to speak. The camera gave me a great chance to see it in close up. This excited me terribly. Working with close up gave me the opportunity to really play with an idea. I felt that close up gave a viewing experience similar to that of viewing large paintings in a church. From a distance, they're designed to impress. Working close up gave me the chance to be God and play with this viewing experience.

In *Bite* you have the image of an apple. This connects to the snake and primary sin, but in the film that all boils down to the image of a beautiful pair of lips biting an apple. Eroticism is a great issue; there are positive and negative images that relate to it. For me it was important to frame the body very close. Remember, society was even more sexist at that time. Think of Allen Jones' work, which was considered 'fun'. Pornography could not be sold legally; it could only be received by mail, mostly from Sweden, but if discovered it was considered illegal material. Pornography depersonalises and fragments a person: it breaks the body down to very small specific parts. It was important to me as a feminist, with very strong feelings about this, to make artistic statements that 'reinstated' the human body. The word *votive*, the title of one of the films, means 'sacred offering'.

Leda Papaconstantinou, *The Box*, 1981, photograph by Erricos Meliones.

The Box

A white box 150 x 400 x 150 cm, occupied the middle of the exhibition space; it was divided in three sections: On the left was a black room, 150 x 150 x 150 cm. In the middle was a red room, 150 x 100 x 150 cm. On the right was a white room, 150 x 150 x 150 cm. The interior of the rooms was visible through viewer lenses placed on the sides of the box. Wooden spools and blue ceramic hearts littered the floor around it and the spectators trod on them in order to reach the box and peep through the lenses. Behind the box hung a large wooden crown with rusty old fixtures for electric bulbs; a relic from times of monarchy. On either side of the crown old documents of female labor were mounted, time sheets, letters of discipline, and photographs of a woman embroidering on a kerchief. She was standing in the ruins of the factory that once produced cotton spools. We lived inside the box for four hours daily. I lived in the white room and my colleague Lesley Walton lived in the black one. Each built her environment according to her needs. Sometimes we met in the red room to perform short actions. We mostly used red clothes and accessories. On one occasion only Lesley lay on the floor and I slowly covered her nearly naked body with white daisies. Her room had two opposing mirror walls, a tape recorder with two pairs of earphones that she shared with the spectators. A super-8 projector occasionally projected a landscape film on her body. My room contained a multitude of objects, mostly of personal value: letters, photos, books, shoes, a small mattress, Christmas lights, a mirror, a knife, a chopping board. The ceiling was covered with paper boats made of folded photocopies showing a group of young women, my grandmother and her friends in the early 1900s. Most of the time we performed in isolation. Our passive availability contrasted with the attitude of active voyeurism that the spectators exhibited. Three times we performed out of the box. These performances are described separately.

Leda Papaconstantinou

Leda Papaconstantinou, *Dim Landscape*, 1982, photograph by Alexis Stamatiadis.

Dim Landscape

The audience walks into a soft circular room made of flesh coloured foam rubber, through a vertical slit of red satin lips; they enter a deep red, womb-like space and sit on the floor. Dim light. Facing them at the far end sit **three Working Women** with their instruments: a cotton mattress, a pile of feathers, three pillowcases. A large red woven fabric hangs on the curved wall. On their left stands a low naked bed with spring wires and a starched white pillow. Behind the bed is a back-lit screen; hidden under the bed are seven glass saucers containing paper castles. On a pedestal poses **a Handsome Man** in formal dress; seven champagne glasses hang from the ceiling, and a champagne bottle is by his feet. His posture resembles that of James Bond, without a gun. Behind him stand **two Flashers** in grey coats and hats. To their right another woman: **the Viola Player.** By the Handsome Man sits the Narrator, dressed in many layers of red clothes which she ceremoniously removes throughout the narration. She is surrounded by piles of pocketbook romances, icons and almond candy. She holds three texts in her lap: Genesis, Death, and Altamura: the story of an artist. **The Machinist,** a knitting machine operator, coordinates the performance: I keep the pace by rhythmically tapping my foot to the sound of the machine. Near the audience, on the floor, is a semicircle of white sand. Lights off. The voice of a little girl is heard singing a song. Enters **an 11-year-old Girl,** dressed in a white frock, and sits on the bed. She holds a silver hammer. Viola Player plays briefly. I start to operate the knitting machine. Workers do their chores, unraveling the red fabric, gutting the mattress, stuffing the pillowcases with feathers. Handsome fills up a glass with champagne. Young Girl breaks his glass with her hammer, and returns to the bed. Narrator reads a long list from Genesis: 'Adam gave birth to Seth, Seth gave birth to Enoch …' Flashers move forward as one, expose themselves to the Women, and walk backwards to their starting point. Viola plays. Handsome fills another glass and poses. Enter **Lover and Bureaucrat,** pulling behind them **Ballerina** who poses on a little trolley; they place her inside the semicircle of sand. Lifting up her arms they tie them with red ribbons suspended from the ceiling. Lover is bare-breasted, in a white suit, white face and heavy makeup. Bureaucrat wears grey flannels and white long sleeves, his face grey in colour. Narrator recites quotations from romances, each one ending with the phrase: '… and their eyes met' while removing items of her clothing. Young Girl breaks yet another glass. Flashers expose themselves. Handsome refills. Viola plays short phrases. Women work. Machinist operates. Lover sleeks his hair back with a green comb, looks in the hand mirror and puts lipstick on. Bureaucrat brushes his nails, takes a stamp and ink out of his pockets. They both proceed to work on Ballerina, covering her naked arms, back and throat with stamps and kisses. They finish and exit holding hands. Death text begins: 'Juliet died of love … Ophelia died of love … Unknown died of love … Antigone died of love …' Young Girl places the saucers on the sand around Ballerina, sprinkles them first with glitter, then with spirits, and sets them alight. Working Women stop their work, walk to Ballerina, untie the ribbons, carry her to the bed, and place her gently on it. They resume their travail. Flashers flash to the reclining Ballerina. Recitation of Altamura's story that culminates with her birth date: 'Spetses 1824'. It is accompanied by a shadow-play on the screen. Viola ceases to play as the screen goes black. Narrator removes her socks and exits, followed by Workers. Machinist plays her mechanical tune, stops, then starts anew. For the first time Flashers turn to face the audience, and stop right in front of them. They expose themselves. The mirrors covering their genitals reflect the faces of the people. Young Girl smashes the mirrors with her silver hammer. Blackout.

Leda Papaconstantinou

Leda Papaconstantinou, *Bouboulitsa's Dream*, 1979, photograph by Dimitris Papadimas.

Bouboulitsa's Dream

Where the Sun and the Rain, angry with the Spetsiots, go on a strike. Their anger is justified. Tourism and easy money-making has degraded people's attitudes towards their community. Issues about environment, healthcare, sanitation, and traffic are forgotten. With neither sunshine nor rain, business collapses, still, people remain passive and indifferent. Bouboulitsa's best girlfriend, the Ant, a renowned historian is hit by a Wild Motorbike and breaks a few arms. She needs medical care (not provided on the island) and must be transported to Athens. The Wind and the Sea are playing chase, so no boats are running. The TV Weatherman advises Bouboulitsa to negotiate with the Sun and the Rain. She discusses the problem with her friends, the insects, and off she goes to meet the Forces, carried by the Southern Wind. They receive her kindly and present her with a riddle: the islanders must remember a magic word, long forgotten. The word SPETSES is recollected and all ends well. Each letter (in Greek) is the initial for lovely words, like: love, compassion, pride, respect, equality, freedom. Even the Rat, the Cockroach and the Pig were invited to the party organized by Bouboulitsa's friends, the Butterfly, the Dung Beetle, two Lady Birds, two Baby Beetles, a TV Weatherman, and an Ant.

Leda Papaconstantinou

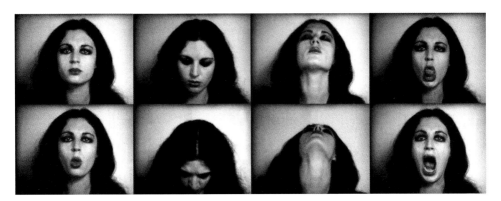

Oh Godard {1969} (Celebrating Godard, Self Portrait)
Directed and filmed by Leda Papaconstantinou. Super 8mm, colour, silent loop, duation: 4':10"
Performer: Leda Papaconstantinou.

Following page: installation view with
photographs by Peter Moore in foreground, see
list of titles on pages 153–154.

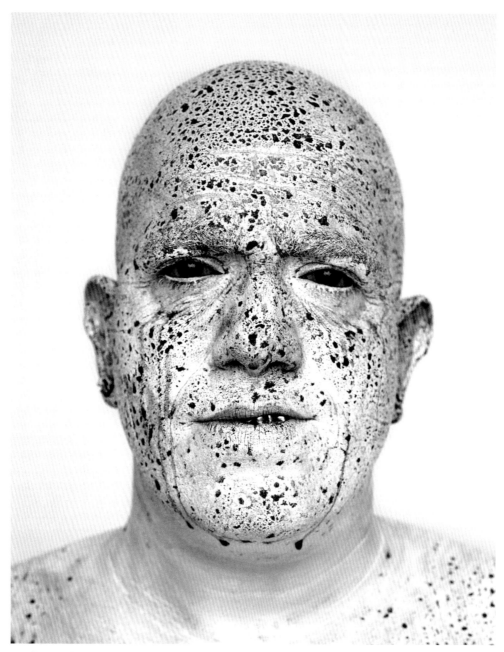

Franko B and Manuel Vason, *Collaboration #8*, London 2003.

PHOTOGRAPHS FROM MANUEL VASON'S ENCOUNTERS

Alice Maude-Roxby

While leafing through publications (still by far the predominant way one comes to know about performance art), the viewer participates in a sort of narrative. Unlike an ideal "documentary" narrative, however, this story unwinds in ways that may not be anticipated. In fact, the viewer's experience is one of a narrative-in-reverse. An unconscious haptic response is mobilized as the viewer touches a photograph taken by a photographer who touched the trigger of the camera as the performer touched his or her own skin, used his or her own body both as an instrument of touch and as performance material. This chain of experience, working backward in time, subtly locks the viewer into a metaphoric complicity with the photographer/viewer, as well as with the performer. These links recreate the largely tacit bond that allowed the performer's action to be played out in the first place. The photograph thus becomes a pseudolegal form of "proof" (term relating photography to law) that an agreement took place.[1]

Kathy O'Dell

Manuel Vason's photographs have appeared in a wide range of diverse publications, on the pages of magazines such as *i-D* and *Dazed and Confused*, as well as in his self-initiated, highly illustrated publications *Exposures*[2] and *Encounters*[3]. These books offer a substantial visual overview of contemporary performance in the UK at present. The photographs published therein are the results of a particular collaborative process established between Vason and a number of contemporary performance artists. Franko B, Ron Athey and Ernst Fischer are key protagonists with whom Vason has worked over years, but he has also intentionally chosen to work with artists whose practices have received less exposure. Much of the work recorded is 'high-risk', and involves pushing the body to its physical and sensual limits or situating the body in particular contexts that test out its vulnerabilities. Having extensively documented public performances Vason identified that restrictions were imposed upon his process through the fact that a live audience was present. He began to extend the period of recording to include the time immediately prior to and following the public event so that he could work without the audience. In order to further this process of working with performance artists outside of scheduled public events, Vason independently raised funding both for high quality

Gwendoline Robin and Manuel Vason, *Collaboration #1, Brussels*, 2006.

Gwendoline Robin and Manuel Vason, *Collaboration #2, Brussels*, 2006.

Richard Hancock & Traci Kelly and Manuel
Vason, *Collaboration #1*, Nottingham, 2004.

Richard Hancock & Traci Kelly and Manuel
Vason, *Collaboration #3*, Nottingham 2004.

production, which would result in large format colour Polaroid photographs and for the publications through which the resultant works could
be disseminated. In Vason's case his particular mode of 'performance to
camera' through which the photographs evolve, involves an intense period
of collaboration with the artist pictured. In this collaboration, drawing
from the conceptual and aesthetic vocabulary associated with the artist's
practice, a new work is realised. The collaboration variously extends from
the ideas, and decisions regarding the locations at which the work is photographed, to the making of props or objects activated within the images.
The photographs subsequently have a shared copyright between Vason and
each of the individual artists. The issue of copyright in relation to the
history of performance and its documentation is extremely complex and
can be problematic: from both sides artists and photographers have at
times blocked each other's permission to publish images.

Footnotes

1. Kathy O'Dell, *Contract with the Skin: Masochism, Performance Art and the
   1970s*, Minneapolis, University of Minnesota Press, 1998, p. 14.
2. Manuel Vason, Ron Athey, Lois Keidan, *Exposures*, Black Dog Publishing, 2002.
3. Manuel Vason, *Encounters*, edited by Dominic Johnson, Arnolfini, 2007.

DOCUMENTATION AND ANA MENDIETA

Hans Breder and Alice Maude-Roxby
April 2006

ALICE MAUDE-ROXBY: Initially it was difficult to trace you as the photographer of some early Ana Mendieta performances. Early publications of performance art do not always credit those who documented the work. Once I found your name I looked at your other work. I am intrigued by your own practice, where Mendieta was sometimes the model, and your documentation of her early works. The Mendieta exhibition catalogue, from the 2004 show at the Hirshhorn curated by Olga Viso, gives context to her early works as a student in the Intermedia programme at Iowa. I understand you set that up in the 1960s; perhaps we could begin there?

HANS BREDER: I founded the Intermedia programme at the University of Iowa in 1968. A visiting artist's project was cornerstone. All my students, including Ana, participated. Robert Wilson, one of the first artists we invited, stayed for a semester. His piece, *Deafman Glance*, evolved through workshops with my students.

From 1969 on, I invited Allan Kaprow, Hans Haacke, Vito Acconci, and others. Willoughby Sharp gave one of the first video presentations of body works. These visiting artists informed my students tremendously regarding contemporary European work. They knew conceptual and performance art from Yves Klein to the Viennese Actionists to Manzoni.

A lot of Ana's early work came out of that teaching environment. The students, visiting artists, and myself all worked in the same loft space outside Iowa City. When the course

started the campus had no studio spaces. The background appearing in many photographs was the wall of our teaching space. Charlie Ray's plank pieces were done against this wall. In one photo you see Ana holding up a chicken in front of the wall (*Untitled (Death of Chicken)*, 1972). In another, you see me cutting the chicken's head off. I did my work against that wall too. That was where we performed.

AMR: I was surprised by these early student works partly because of the professional way they were documented. The photographs break down live action so the piece can read as a sequence of still colour images. They are well composed; the action is well lit. In my experience, this seems far more considerate of the role photography can play in extending the life of an ephemeral event than most students would be aware of.

HB: You have to imagine: this was 1968. Ours was the first MFA of its kind. Intermedia work was very new. I encouraged students to document their work. They needed documentation of ephemeral performances to get their degrees. Otherwise they had nothing to present. I taught that the process for making work included conception of the piece, making it, and final documentation as a photographic sequence. The students were very good about it. I made the importance of documentation clear because I had first-hand experience. Much of my early work wasn't documented or I had

Ana Mendieta, *Imagen de Yagul* 1973.
Lifetime colour photograph.
© The Estate of Ana Mendieta Collection. Courtesy Galerie Lelong.
Photo documentation by Hans Breder. Collection Hans Breder.

a lousy photographer who didn't 'get it'.

I documented Ana's work myself. I worked there beside her: often we worked at the same sites. I recorded some pieces in the classroom and many pieces made in the landscape. I made my own work at the same sites using performers. Often Ana was the performer or model in my work. When I met her, Ana was in the painting programme. By the time she joined my Intermedia class we were already intimate.

For assessment to gain her painting MA, Ana presented photographs where she transfers hair cut from Morty Sklar's moustache and beard to stick onto her own face, (*Untitled (Facial Hair Transplants)*, 1972). She did the piece in our classroom. She progressively glued hair Sklar was cutting from his face onto her own until she had a beard and moustache. Then she walked around town for the rest of the day, going to bars, getting drunk and getting a lot of attention.

AMR: Many of the Mendieta works you documented were made in the landscape. I was interested to read that some were made during her studies in the Intermedia programme.

HB: From the beginning I encouraged students to get out of the classroom. I said, 'Even if this loft is not school, it leads us to create conventions. To break that, get out into the streets, into the landscape, out of the country.' One student made a piece on the central square crossing in Iowa City. He laid a square of salt directly onto the crossing. As pedestrians crossed the roads, the salt smeared. It became a beautiful kind of constructivist drawing.

I extended this idea of working outside the university by travelling with students to other countries. These cross-cultural experiments were key to the programme concept. In 1973, I brought about ten students to Yagul, Mexico. When Ana did her piece I remember there were four or five students around, placed strategically to watch for guards. The guards found us, but got caught up with it and stood and watched. Students were always present at each other's works. Amongst the group there was a give and take. Sometimes one person's work was similar to another's; they learnt from each other as much as they learnt from the visiting artists because they participated in production of the work. That is, of course, the best way of learning.

Yagul is the piece where Ana is covered in flowers we bought at the market. Part of my job was to arrange the flowers on top of her, to look as if they were growing out of her body. In terms of documentation, Ana wanted everything photographed very tight. But after a few photos I would get bored. So what does the photographer do? I moved further back; found new angles. Generally I would shoot a full roll of colour slide film, 36 exposures. I would shoot to get the full sequence, if action was present. Or the piece might take place through changing light. Through the series I would record that change. After the event, keeping complete documentation and the sequence of images together and in order is really important. With works like *Anima, Silhueta de Cohetes*, 1976, there were extreme changes in lighting, from daylight to darkness, and from the unlit construction to the construction being set on fire. When you light something and it gets dark, you also record the traces that are left. Since Ana's death, these sequences have not been kept together. Single images have been printed and shown on their own. All of a sudden you have hundreds of works, because each piece started with 36 photographs. I was supposed to shoot a roll to constitute one work as far as the artist was concerned, but makes thirty-six as far as the market is concerned.

When we split, Ana said, 'Choose two photographs.' I chose the *Tree of Life*

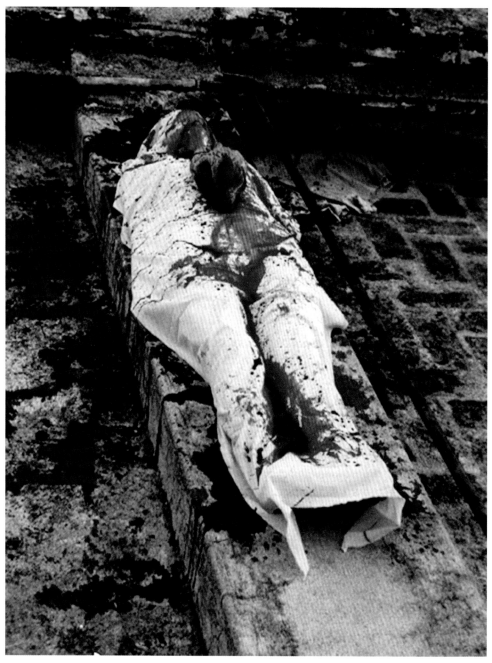

Ana Mendieta, *Untitled*. Hotel Principal, Oaxaca, 1973.
Lifetime colour photograph.
© The Estate of Ana Mendieta Collection. Courtesy Galerie Lelong.
Photo documentation by Hans Breder. Collection Hans Breder.

Hans Breder, *Body Sculpture* (Hotel Principal), 1973.

and *Yagul* in which we had been most collaborative. In *Tree of Life*, 1976, I positioned her against a tree, covered her body in mud, and then photographed the piece. Ana's work translates beautifully into photography. The original action was not always riveting, but the process of photographing transformed the work.

AMR: I noticed that your documentation of her early work is primarily slide film. Was the intention that the translation into photography could result in a time-based presentation?

HB: In some cases yes, for example, the firework piece I spoke about earlier, *Anima, Silhueta de Cohetes*. She worked like this: I drew an outline of her body; in this case onto a piece of paper. We gave the drawing to someone who made fireworks; he created this bundled construction in the shape of her body. We lit it one evening; I turned on my Super 8 camera. It was almost a twilight situation with the view against a mountain. I took one slide after another of every stage. This piece was meant to be seen as a slide display of 36 images. In this case all 36 slides are critical.

AMR: Within a wider survey of how performance documentation has been exhibited or published I notice that different artists choose either to limit documentation just to one image or to publish sequences that give more a sense of how the piece unfolded through time. I particularly like the pieces where there is a sequence of images, and the actuality of the performance can be read. Single images, as documentation of performance, can reinforce an iconic quality which, seen alone, may be interpreted in different ways. They are potentially read as photographs rather than documentation. Separation removes them from context of the whole performance, which you can only see

through the complete sequence.

HB: This is what needs to be talked about.

AMR: Would you say that the Super 8 films give a more complete documentation of the work?

HB: Not really. The films are only three minutes long. A few worked out well, where I put the camera up high in Oaxaca. There was a big boulder; Ana was floating, gasping for air in this creek. I filmed straight down. Setting up to get that shot is crucial.

AMR: How did those decisions come about? Did you discuss the translation of action into photography prior to the event?

HB: It was always discussed. I knew what Ana wanted by that time, and she gave me a free hand. We never planned it. I can't imagine that. For example, the piece on the rooftop of Hotel Principal, in Mexico, where we were staying (*Untitled*, 1973). Earlier we'd gone to the butcher, got blood. Got a cow's heart. Back at the hotel, she ripped off the bed sheet. We went up on the roof. She lay down naked. I arranged the sheet over her body, poured the blood over her, placed the beef heart and took the photographs. Ok? From the moment she lays down it was all in my hands, where do I place the beef heart? She said, 'On my chest'. That's relatively vague.

AMR: The way you describe the spontaneity is really interesting. Some works, like *Untitled (Rape Scene)*, 1973, seem different. With that I was struck by how staged the photographs seem; I also wondered about the lighting.

HB: Ana did that piece in response to a rape on campus. She did the piece as a tableaux at her apartment. She left the door slightly ajar. We came in and saw her tied up, the coat hanger, the blood on the floor. The audience

Hans Breder, *Body Sculpture* (La Ventosa),1973.

was the workshop. In this case the students and everyone in the department were just mingling. Finally we untied her, she cleaned up, we went to a bar, got drunk and talked about it.

She made other pieces to confront the audience. In one there was a little closet, the glass part of the door was painted green. She scraped an area of paint off it and pressed her lips against it. When you came in you saw these distorted lips against the glass. In another piece, Ana was lying in the street in Clinton, Iowa. I was performing inside in the actual space. Ana decided to stay outside and play dead. She was lying in the street with blood coming from her mouth. People would stop and check whether she was alive. There was something melodramatic about Ana that crept into her work.

AMR: Is there an overlap between your own practice and Mendieta's? In some photographic works of yours, you place the body in a landscape with mirrors reflecting both body and landscape.

HB: I would not say that there was overlap in our practices. Ana was my student. She was bright and avaricious. She took and made her own the cornerstones of the Intermedia programme with its emphasis on site-specific performative work. She followed me in my involvement with the body, especially in Mexico and at Old Man's Creek, where we actually worked at the same sites. As artists, what we did have in common was the experience of diaspora. As an artist, Ana wanted to mediate her loss by becoming one with the earth. I, on the other hand, used the body as a liminal, transformative site.

Following page detail: Babette Mangolte, *Looking and Touching*, 2007.

HANDMADE

Babette Mangolte and Alice Maude-Roxby
March 2006

ALICE MAUDE-ROXBY: As you know, in this exhibition I'm concerned with drawing out what different photographers bring to the role of documenting performance. I am thinking of the work of each performance photographer as a translation. This extends from my essay in the Tate Liverpool catalogue where I wrote about photographers, such as yourself and Peter Moore, being present and photographing at the same events but producing entirely different images. Becoming aware of the different attributes that individual photographers brought to the role of recording performance perhaps one can understand more exactly what the performance was. One can then distinguish how the action has been framed by the ideas and aesthetics of the particular photographer.

BABETTE MANGOLTE: Photography is a gesture. More than anything else I valued an instinctive gesture. This was also valued by Rauschenberg and Whitman. The handmade quality of the work of art was really important to the Pop Artists. Bizarrely, you look at Andy Warhol and you think: 'Oh it is totally anonymous', but that is actually not true at all. You look at Warhol's early film and it is totally individualistic in terms of the framing and the camera moves, and you can recognise this in all of the films that were framed by him. With Andy Warhol there's that dandy façade of not caring, but there was real precision behind it. That is also the case with his silkscreens. I was not witness to his process as I met him only later when I arrived in New York in the 1970s. But the handmade gesture is as evident in his silkscreens as it is in his film work.

The same was true of Rauschenberg: I discovered this when I looked at his combines from the 1950s with him while working on a film of his first retrospective in Washington in 1976. When we spoke it was clear that he valued the individualism of who he was when he had made those works a decade earlier. Rauschenberg's art is not conceptual in the sense that the idea pulls everything; the involvement in administering the materiality of the work is really important. And materiality is, of course, what performance is all about. Look at Rauschenberg's blue body prints from 1950. They are completely different from Yves Klein's, which were made by putting paint onto the body. With Rauschenberg's the process had an organic quality about it: this is an imprint of the body where the body is in contact with the photographic paper which records the photogram and turns blue when processed. I think that sense of the handmade, or rather how the handmade is made visible by the personalisation of the touch and sensibility of the maker was important to me in my practice in shooting photographs. I was also fascinated in looking at what I was photographing and my amazement had to be communicated by my photographs. Other photographers covering the same performance actually were not interested in what they were photographing.

AMR: One is aware of your particular 'personalisation' both through the way in which you framed up the photographs and selected moments to shoot, and also through the particularities of processing and printing. You did the darkroom work and printed the photographs yourself, was this unusual?

BM: Oh yes, and it was difficult. I often had to push the film to 800 ASA because there was not enough light, and you had to do it without increasing the grain. It is all in the manual agitation of the film tank while processing. I knew that skill was relevant to make some shots possible. I definitely was ahead of photographers who were not good lab technicians.

In taking the photographs I was interested in modelling and depth. I think photography is essentially a frame; it has to do with volume and the volume helped define the gesture and the weight of the body. I think for Peter Moore it has more to do with a flat surface. To diminish the feeling of space, he often put his camera at an angle and he privileged action taken out of the context of the space. For me the context of the space was defining everything and so it was as important to capture as the gestures.

I thought that the photographs should exist because they could be useful for the future, and in the present they were helping me understand what I had seen. I was not particularly interested in how well the photograph could be reproduced. I was concerned with recording light conditions even though underexposed photographs are tricky, too dark, and do not reproduce well in newspapers. I never felt that my photographs' reason to exist was to provide good copy for newspapers; there were very few newspapers reproducing performance photographs anyway. For example, my photograph of Robert Whitman's use of green light is typical of a photograph that would never have been produced by a professional photographer interested purely in shooting for newspapers. The green light photograph is about a transitional event and professionals were just not interested, but for me it was important to understand what the performance was really about. For instance, the photograph of Jim jumping from the ladder was an action revealed by a flash in a brief moment. The audience only saw this image of Jim's jump when the flash, in a small fraction of a second, exposed it out of darkness. The photographs were useful to understand the event after it was past because the photographs could be studied at length. I feel that photography's main achievement is this ability to stop time so we can look and see.

In the mid-1980s the demands for photographs changed. Documentation was done on video and photographs were used for publicity and headshots. There were increasing restrictions about shooting during rehearsal in the actual physical space where the performance was taking place. And there was more demand for colour and good quality colour cannot be obtained in low light and in a mixed colour balance environment. The only way to get good colour was to use a flash and for me that was the end of any kind of three-dimensionality. The flash flattens. Even if you are very skilled and you use a strobe and you don't have the flash attached to the camera body you can only obtain a certain limited three-dimensionality. I didn't want to get equipped for that, I lost interest because of it. So that was the end of it. I was more interested in making film; there is a certain dissatisfaction in constantly producing photographs of performance. People may think you are good and look at the photographs and tell you they are great. They are pleased that the images exist but they don't do anything with them. These photographs are never really looked at more than once.

AMR: Earlier we talked about Andy Warhol and a kind of understated signature, which is given to the objects through their being made by hand. Although he may have given the impression of being 'hands off' with the relationship to the work he made, if you look closely you see how incredibly particular he was regarding the objects' materiality. With that in mind I realise that I am looking at the photographs you have made as objects, the physicality of which is entirely different from viewing hardcopy digital files of documentation of contemporary performance. I'm looking at black and white photographs and contact prints, which also show traces of their making as well as making evident a selection process. I think that for the artists whose performances are pictured these photographs are in their own right very good objects which, through the particularities of their physicality and the now outdated processes they evidence, anchor each performance event to the particular time it was made.

BM: At the time it is true that the convention was that one good photograph could carry what the performance was all about. For me retrospectively I think that concept was somewhat reactionary and reductive. It presupposes that the performance can be seen from a purely objective point of view. It minimises the subjectivity of the spectator and his immediate reaction to the event as well as the context. And I think context is really important in performance, especially the context of how the performance is perceived by the spectator. I always tried to shoot photographs that show the spectator's perception of the performance. Is it why you now think those photos are more like object than documents?

In the 1970s photography and film were both mute. No sound is attached to the visual photographic record and in the 1970s film was also mute. To record film with

sound would have required more expensive equipment that nobody had, not even Rauschenberg. He had a noisy 16 mm camera he used for himself and also lent to his friends like Yvonne Rainer and Bob Whitman. Film shot then was thought of as fragments. When Bob Whitman filmed for his performance work he thought of isolated images and movements that would be integrated into the live performance, like in *Prune Flat*, one of his most extraordinary performances. *Prune Flat* was originally staged in 1965 but has been restaged several times by Bob Whitman and in particular in 2002 at Centre Georges Pompidou in Paris. The museum bought the copyright of the performance and made a DVD, a beautiful restaging by Whitman with the projected film made with Rauschenberg's camera in 1965 and featuring Simone Forti and Lucinda Childs. The film shot on Kodachrome is very beautiful and its colours have not faded. It was shot first and projected onto the same performers dressed in white in Jonas Mekas's movie theatre in 1965. The white of the costume acted as a screen. You see in the photographs I made of the first reconstruction in 1976 how the 1965 film is projected onto a different cast on stage. You perceive the projection through the shadow cast by the beam of one of the film projectors projecting the background onto the stage while a second film projector projected onto the white dresses of the performers on stage. In analysing the photos you can see the double projection that was not obvious to the spectator. We can see it when the projectionist put his finger in front of the lens to create that area of shadow. You see the person in front and discover there is a double projection: the background projection with this shadow, and the projection of another image which is putting clothes on that woman, or projecting a naked body onto that other woman dressed in a white smock, like a nurse's gown. What you saw in *Prune Flat* was strange and fascinating to decode. You never knew if you were seeing a projection or the real thing. Here Simone appears to be actually floating, that was shot in the actual movie and projected amongst people who were standing. I absolutely adore those photographs that are a 1960s version of 'trompe l'oeil'!

AMR: Currently re-enacting early performances seems to be the preferred mode for re-examining those works. Re-enactment raises an interesting dilemma about the status of the original documentation both as information for restaging but also in the way the original documentation connects through the particularities of the media available, such as the aesthetics of Kodachrome you described, in the era of the initial performance. I was really interested that you made the film *Four Pieces by Morris* in 1993 of performances Robert Morris originally made in the 1960s. In conceiving the film you addressed the questions of how to bring the performances into the present, could you tell me more about that process?

BM: Yes, I felt that for a film to succeed in this way you really needed stylisation. With photography you can stylise immediately, even in the present tense because you see the things for the first time. Somehow the frame shows the photographer's eye and brings forward a formal presentation of what you represent. In film it is much more difficult if you are involved in just documenting performance work. 'Can you really frame the event with the proper perspective?' 'Can you find the proper distance?' I think it is much more difficult to document live with film than it is after the act. If you can re-enact with the performers and the camera you have better control and you can vary the distance at which you look at the unfolding event. Film has to structure the way the film spectator looks at the event and how his perception evolves during the performance. You need time to think before filming. When you shoot off the cuff, which is what I did with Marina Abramović's *Seven Easy Pieces*, I had little control. But I was so conscious of the problem that I studied Marina's work in depth before shooting *Seven Easy Pieces*, which had to be shot in the moment of the action at the Guggenheim Museum and therefore could not be restaged after the weeklong event. I realised I had to be as instinctive and reactive shooting the film as I had been in the past when shooting photographs.

AMR: You said that everybody hated your film of Robert Morris, what was so provocative about it?

BM: People who had seen the performance in 1963 or 1965 were saying, 'It was not like that!' They remembered spaghetti cable all over the place, and it was dirty and not nicely lit. So they hated the film and I remember feeling that it was completely fitting that they should hate it because they wanted to get back to their youth and that was absolutely not what it was about for me! Who cares! The film was made for people like me who hadn't seen the work in the 1960s. I felt that what had to be communicated was a sense of time and not a facsimile of what had been photographed in the 1960s. I think film encapsulates time for a given period. Bob Morris was really happy with the film. I put a lot of money and effort into the sound. Bob was sceptical but he said, 'You are the filmmaker, you decide'. I felt that time and duration would be carried through the sound and it was important to shoot sync, to record the sound of Andrew's body panting while manipulating the plywood. The sound of the performer's body is taken for granted when the performance is taking place in front of you live. Spectators don't realise how important the sensation of seeing 'live' is and how it has to be recreated in the film.

Barbara Clausen

When I saw Adrian Piper's 1976 collage *This is not the Documentation of a Performance* for the first time, the full impact that the documentation and mediatisation of performances has on its fundamental claim to authenticity became apparent. Every photograph, video, and film that has remained in circulation in the past decades is more than a mere historical document. It is also the presentation, staging, visual object, and trace of the event and the era it took place in. Piper's reproduction of a grainy, black and white press image titled 'squatters fight eviction by church' depicts a group of people gathered in a picket line protesting against the loss of their homes in front of the neo-gothic St. John the Divine Cathedral on New York's Upper West Side. The press photo's composition is clearly aimed at evoking emotions. A younger and an older woman are positioned on the right and left sides of the image, while a young man and two children staring into the camera stand between them. Piper replaced the text on one of their protest signs with the sentence 'This is not a Performance.' This seemingly minimal intervention does not disrupt the image-text relation composed by the news photographer. The typeset is consistent with that of the other signs, but the words themselves are addressed to an art audience. The sentence's adaptation of the piece's title, 'This is not the Documentation of a Performance', marks the media status of the image as an index of the event. Piper's message is not only an institutional critique of the real estate market, municipal policy, and the Catholic Church in New York City. She also criticises the expectations and prejudices of the viewers, who, whether it is a day, a few months, or years later, will always consider the collage an exclusively artistic image, thereby absolving themselves from their political responsibility.

Like no other genre, performance art stands for the liberation of traditional power structures and gender relations in the arts and society at large. The ostensible equilibrium between everyday life and art becomes the expression and metaphor of political and emancipatory desires determined by a permutating process of production, representation, and reception. Our understanding of performativity has evolved from perception to communication, from the social to the physical, and from referentiality to indexicality. Performance art's inherent tension lies between the need for action and institutionalisation as well as hyper-mediality and the desire for immediate experience. The analysis of the historically determined binarity of the genre makes it necessary to examine the interference of an ontologically defined Postmodernism and the epistemological discourse of Modernism. In this paper, I will use historical and contemporary works by Adrian Piper, Babette Mangolte, Trisha Brown, Peter Weibel, VALIE EXPORT, Sharon Hayes, Gianni Motti, and Santiago Sierra as examples to illustrate the political potential of performance art and its strategies of mediation.[1] I will investigate how performance art's claim to authenticity was constituted from the 1960s onwards and what has caused its revival in the last decade. The aim is to question the dialogistical nature of the boundaries between art and everyday life by analysing the dynamics and strategies of mediatisation inherent in performance art. In his theory of 'The Emancipated Spectator', Jaques Rancière suggests that the aim is to blur the boundaries and dissolve the opposition between the activity of the performers and the passivity of the audience. However, this should not 'lead to a kind of "hypertheater", turning spectatorship into activity by turning representation into presence'.[2] As the following examples will show, the intrinsic dichotomy in performance art between original and copy, event and reproduction, and performer and spectator can be overcome by activating and emancipating what is thought to be passive.

'Squatters' fight eviction by church

N.Y.C. squatters and supporters demonstrate Jan. 30 outside St. John the Devine church.

The pending eviction of 30 mostly Hispanic families was protested Jan. 30 in front of the Cathedral of St. John the Divine, the New York City church that is trying to force the people out of their homes.

The 30 families served with eviction notices live in one of three buildings on Manhattan's upper west side that have been occupied by the tenants for the last six and one-half years. The Morningside Housing Corp., a coalition of churches in the area led by St. John's, has been trying since 1970 to tear down the tenements and build a high-rise home for the elderly on the site.

The threatened families and their supporters who demonstrated outside the immense cathedral demanded that low-income housing for persons of all ages

be constructed on the site, explained Juan Esdel, one of the tenants facing eviction.

The removal of the working-class residents has been fought in court over the years, but the Episcopalian cathedral has now obtained an eviction order that can be carried out anytime after Feb. 2. "We're not leaving," Esdel declared. "We'll stay and fight — we've learned how to do that. This time we'll fight harder."

After picketing outside the cathedral, the families entered the church during the Sunday service. The minister, in the midst of his sermon, said St. John's was not to blame for the evictions. He then led the congregation in a prayer for the poor.

Adrian Piper, *This is not the Documentation of a Performance*, 1976, © Adrian Piper Research Archive/ Collection.

Trisha Brown, *Accumulation*, at McGraw Hill, New York City, 1973, photograph ©
Babette Mangolte.

The starting point is always the performer's body, changing from a self-
determined and autonomous entity into an activist one. Similar to Piper's
image-text collage, the body amalgamates codes and gestures, which
are discernible independent of the spectator's social background. Thanks
to the abundance of images distributed by mass media, we are equally
familiar with images of people gathering to witness a public spectacle as
with those of anonymous art performances in the context of political demonstrations. In other words, does the perception of a political performance
in public space differ from a performance taking place during a political
demonstration? When, in 1972, a group of Trisha Brown's dancers lay
down in the middle of McGraw shopping plaza in New York City in order
to perform the minimalist choreography of *Accumulation*, an interested
crowd quickly gathered. The presence of the performers' bodies questions
the boundaries of society and the present. The audience and the dancers
are joined together in the moment of their meeting, thus fulfilling the
fundamental intention of street performances. In the ensuing documentations and staging of a performance's images, the political dimension gains
even more momentum than in the immediate event. The photographer,
in this case Babette Mangolte, reveals the interrelation of the dancers'
bodies and the spectators. A comparison of the photographs of Brown's
Accumulation with those of a group of women, clad and painted white,
in a demonstration against the Vietnam War in downtown Manhattan,
reveals the relational difference between the movement dynamics of the
situation and its staging in the image. The image sequence of Mangolte's
contact sheets not only exemplifies her ability to respond quickly, but
also illustrates the influence of cinematography on the rhythm of her

Demonstration on the street in Downtown New York City, photograph © Babette Mangolte, 1972.

movements in relation to the crowd. Whether it is still or moving, the camera is present and positioned to capture the event itself, while also representing the function and role of the audience in the image. Thus, it addresses the reciprocal inscription of the performers and spectators. The boundaries of the subjective experience of a performance cannot be constituted in its immediate experience and the subsequent exchange of both sides, but rather develop in the process of the performance's reception.

The performers' intention to pursue direct interaction with the audience, rejecting the mechanisms of reproduction, can be contested, because what we perceive as 'live' is always subject to mediatisation. In the words of Philip Auslander this means 'to understand the relationship between live and mediatized forms ... as historical and contingent, not as ontologically given or technologically determined. ... The live is actually an effect of mediatization'.[3]

Nonetheless, 'having been there' remains a claim of authenticity that is firmly embedded in the collective perception of performance art. Chroniclers and witnesses are most often the ones who claim the immaterial authenticity of the genre and rival with the performer's status. At first glance, VALIE EXPORT's body action 'TAPP-und TASTKINO' (TAP and TOUCH CINEMA) from 1968 seems to focus on a direct confrontation with the audience. By protesting against 'the film apparatus as a materialized bourgeois ideology'[4] she visualises the divergence between the desires and expectations of the audience and the performer. EXPORT strapped a simple box to her bare chest and walked along the streets of Munich, inviting people to 'visit' the 'cinema' with their hands for a few moments. The female body was transformed into a screen, into film bereft of the sense of seeing, but expanded by the sense of touch. Her accomplishment lies in the questioning of the passive reception of the media and the relation between medium and body in relation to herself and the spectators. Despite the ostensible involvement of her audience, EXPORT's main intent was not to create participation, but rather to analyse the power of the gaze, which is transferred to the mediatised body and its means of representation by the recording and rendering apparatus. Subsequently, the photos, videos, and films brought into circulation perpetuate what is staged in documentation and what is documented in staging, regardless of the artist's actionist or political intention.

The historical and immanent reference and ideological refusal performance art harbours towards its conditions of reproduction becomes part of its visual politics and mediation. Becoming a *dispositif* of its time, the collective imaginary of what performance art stands for increasingly merges with its historical contemplation. Digital as well as analogue recording media have transformed the documentation of performance into a substitute and virtual equivalent of the depicted event. Distribution strategies of documentations and ephemera of all sorts have turned out to guarantee performance art's status and have enabled it to remain firmly embedded as a symbol of social change in collective cultural memory. In a seemingly spontaneous action in 1971, Peter Weibel pulled a piece of paper with the word *lügt* (lies) out of his trench coat, held it up under the sign of a police station in Vienna, and let the photographer take a picture of him, creating the sentence *Polizei lügt* (The police lie.). This subversive intervention only becomes a performance through the reception of its documentation. Compared to the idea of a purely ontological documentation of perform-ance, the concepts of performativity in these works indicated before their time that the documentation of an event as a performance constitutes it as such.[5]

A further early example of performance art's awareness of its own me-diatisation and political impact is Suzanne Lacy's and Leslie Labowitz's performance *In Mourning and in Rage*. In their manifest 'Feminist Media Strategies for Political Performance', the artists questioned and openly protested the media's role in creating a culture of the spectacular. In December 1977, Los Angeles was waiting for news about the Hillside Strangler. The media coverage of the case sensationalised and criminal-ised the lives of the female victims, creating an atmosphere of fear and prejudice. Lacy and Labowitz decided to turn the tables and use the com-municative force of the mass media to present an alternative interpreta-tion of the case. '[It was about] creating a public ritual of rage as well as grief. A motorcade of sixty women followed a hearse to City Hall, where news media reporters waited. Ten very tall women robed in black mourn-ing climbed from the hearse. At the front steps of City Hall, the perform-ers each spoke of a different form of violence against women, connecting these as part of a fabric of social consent for such crimes ... The perform-ance reached its target with extensive coverage on local and statewide news.'[6] In their fight against violence against women in society and the media, *In Mourning and in Rage* proved to be one of Lacy and Labowitz's most successful media performances at the time. The documentation material, consisting of texts, images, and press clippings, represents their intervention in publications in and out of the art context up to this day.

The artists discussed here share a specific focus on the role mediatisa-tion plays in the development of their performances, equally before and after the act. They reflect on a conceptual level how performance art's journey – from 'the event on the street' to 'the image on the wall' – under-goes a series of perspective changes and physical shifts. It is this specific translational displacement from the 'live' to its mediatisation that re-mains a key question in art, performance, and media theory. Describing the way we historically relate to performances from the past as a displace-ment of haptic experience, Kathy O'Dell argues that this displacement constitutes the paradigmatic shift from an ontological event to an epis-temological process, influencing our awareness of the body and physical experience since the 1970s.[7] She specifically links this displacement to 'the socio-political conditions of the 1970s, the decade in which this art form was named and photographic documentation burgeoned'.[8] Using the documentation of performance art to explore the haptic experience of

Peter Weibel, *Polizei lügt, Wien / Police Lies*, Vienna, 1971 from the series *Korrekturen*. Courtesy of Peter Weibel.

Sharon Hayes, *In the near future – Vienna*, 2005–2006. Courtesy of Sharon Hayes.

past events reveals how we relate to that which we have not experienced firsthand. These past and present performances and their heightened awareness of the cultural politics of mediation teach us what an experience of evidences can mean in an increasingly performative environment.

Since the mid-1990s performance art has been experiencing a revival, causing a steady stream of live events to appear in public and non-profit spaces as well as galleries, museums, and art fairs. There are several reasons for this trend. One is to frame our present day understanding of the 'political in art' and to find new means of expression in direct reaction to current social and political issues, such as the war in Iraq, neo-liberal politics of globalisation, or the greenhouse effect. This immediate emancipatory desire is led and fed by a nostalgia for a cultural environment of the 1960s and 1970s, marked by the sometimes romantic desire for revolution and social change.[9] Another lies in theory: what seemed forgotten in the theoretical debate on cultural memory for nearly three decades, reemerged a decade ago in the paradigmatic shift of the 'performative turn'. Art plays a vital role in the dialectic of historical amnesia and memory. The appearance of performativity in art history, cultural studies, and critical theory has kept the discussion about the ontological origins of performance art in light of modern day media alive. At the same time theory started to have its effect on current art practices, the rediscovery of past performance art began gaining commercial value and finding its way into private and public collections. The upsurge of performance art's symbolical value is tightly linked to its growing commercial value, which has increased notably through private as well as institutional acquisitions.[10] A vast array of exhibitions and symposiums on the subject, such as the exhibition and publication at hand, continuously perpetuate and investigate these developments. The growing relevance of performativity in politics, economy, theory, and art has provoked not just new initiatives, but also an infinite number of revivals and appropriations. Caught in the middle of this participatory strive for effect, we find ourselves surrounded by ephemera and re-enactments, blurring the boundaries of nostalgic historicization, market-friendly acquisition, and subversive appropriation. It has become apparent that both the political as well as the institutional currents in performance art incorporate and translate a desire for an idealised past into the present and future. It is this shared affinity for the immediate experience and the potential of communicative exchange that makes Relational Aesthetics a forerunner and parallel movement to performance art's revival. Their sequential popularity in the art world has proven equally susceptible to recent criticism. As the past decade has shown, their shared claim as democratic and political forms of art, neither can nor will break free from the art context and its market-driven structures through direct contact with their audience.[11] If not addressed directly, the de-contextualisation of performance art, as an object or an event, runs the risk of losing its past and present agency.

Today, performance art is not just a genre, but a tool amongst many to deal with the world. A generation of artists is using performance as a method to address the translational quality and history inherent to performance art as an artistic strategy. Despite the differences in their approaches, these artists – in full awareness of their own and others' bodies – use social realities and conditions as well as historical facts in their common goal of questioning given structures. The following examples of Sharon Hayes', Gianni Motti's, and Santiago Sierra's work will highlight the different ways the performative presence of their selves and others are used as a tool in relation to media for their investigations of the manifold relationship society and art take on.

Hayes's conscious display of her 'investigative gaze into the past' is essential for her attempt to make the political dimension of the 'here and now' graspable. Her 2006 performance series and installation *In the near future – Vienna,*[12] is part of her ongoing investigation of protest, consisting of a series of anachronistic and speculative actions in public space. For a period of seven days, Hayes went to different locations in Vienna with different protest signs. Each of the slogans referred to a protest that had taken place in the respective location. The audience was invited to document her actions, rather then just observe. After each day their photographs would be installed and presented as a steadily growing collection of slides and viewpoints on the one-woman demonstration. Their participatory labor justified Hayes' presence in the public sphere, each day marking each other's translational achievements. In the installation, the images became agents of her singular political action. While investigating the power of past protests and their relationship to public space in the immediate presence, her conceptual installation becomes an archival investigation of her plural role as artist and activist. When historical events achieve a new topicality, they often undergo a temporal and spatial shift caused by the immediate reaction of the audience, collective memory, and the assumption that the event had been forgotten. Hayes investigates the border between art and activism by entwining their different forms of mediation with active and passive spectatorship.

Performance art's capability to serve as an ideological index may stem from the immediate participation of the audience and other forms of interaction on a micro level, but its full potential is rather situated in the process of transcription to different media and communicative distribution systems. Today the understanding of what a political public is and the incorporation of art in its sphere is different than at the time of *In Mourning and in Rage* or *TAPP und TASTKINO*. What happens when Motti launches an attack on the harsh reality of the media and Sierra (ab)uses the bodies of people oppressed and marginalised by society? How do works like these challenge the art world's self-asserted claim of critically examining the socio-political structures of our time?

In the wake of the Abu Ghraib scandal, Motti pulled a black plastic bag over his head at the 2004 French Open tennis tournament, immediately attracting the attention of all cameras present and thus blurring the boundaries between artistic staging, voyeurism, and subversive intervention. While keeping a close reign on the representation of text and image information within his installations, Motti gives up the power and the rights over his image in the mass media. Whereas Lacy and Labowitz strove to establish a lasting cooperation with the media in order to induce social change and spread public awareness, Motti initiated his contact to the media by forcefully superimposing his physical presence into the camera shots. At the same time, dispersing accounts of his action in the form of news images, documentations, and anecdotes, became more important for the constitution of the performance than provoking an immediate reaction by the present audience. The initial staging of the image completely eludes his control in the present as well as the future.

Similar to Motti, Sierra works with the effect produced by the collision of reality and power relations, thus creating a stark contrast to the seemingly sublime palladium of art. In his performances and installations, cause, intention, and empathy are not presented as ideological antagonisms or successive sequences. Sierra rather understands them as equal levels of meaning with different modes of reception, which already overlap during the production process. In actions such as *133 persons paid to have their hair dyed blonde* from 2001 he reveals the core structures of our society and the mechanisms of economy and community. Sierra intentionally translates the inhuman and humiliating side of the economic system into the context of the museum, whether in live performances or as documentations of his work. His explorations concentrate on testing the borders of the institutionalised framework, one which has always managed to incorporate and thus neutralise even the most subversive artistic strategies. Reversing the subversive potential of performance art from the outside back into the inside of the system.

Despite the apparent differences and attitudes in their performances, Hayes, Motti, and Sierra share a desire to address the divergence between the incapability to leave the cultural sphere and its at times powerful potential as a social index. The premise for the exploration of this ideological gap lies in the conscious integration of the discontinuities, expectations, failures, and ruptures that are usually edited out in the process of performance arts' historicization. Recording, in other words, what leads to a loss of memory, yet remains as invisible markers that establish the mediation of performance art. By doing so these artists make visible the values, norms, and structures of a daily life, built on the contingent relationship between the media and the immediate. Performance art today has the power to question the privileged status of the live presence, making it 'a matter of linking what one knows with what one does not know, of being at the same time performers who display their competences and spectators who are looking to find what those competences might produce in a new context, among unknown people'.[13] It is within this counter-reflective exchange that 'a new stage of equality can be reached'[14] and different kinds of performative acts, as part of daily life, bear the potential to be translated and counter read with each another.

Essay translated and edited by Margarethe Clausen.

Footnotes

1. This also includes works that seem to not be politically motivated at first glance. Despite their ostensible antagonism, they can always be considered signs of their time, whether they are expressive or commercial spectacles.
2. Jaques Rancière, 'The Emancipated Spectator', *Artforum*, March 2007, p. 280 'The Emancipated Spectator' was originally presented in English at the opening of the Fifth International Summer Academy of Arts in Frankfurt on August 20, 2004. The text appeared in *Artforum* in a slightly revised form.
3. Philip Auslander, *Liveness: Performance in a Mediatized Culture*, Routledge, London/New York, 1999, p. 51.
4. Sabine Breitwieser (ed.), *Occupying Space: Collection Catalogue Generali Foundation*, Generali Foundation, Vienna, 2003, p. 82.
5. See essay by Philip Auslander in Barbara Clausen (ed.): *The (Re)Presentation of Performance Art*, Verlag Moderner Kunst, Nürnberg, 2006. pp. 21–34, p. 27.
6. Suzanne Lacy and Leslie Labowitz, 'Feminist Media Strategies for Political Performance', published in Jan Cohen-Cruz (ed.), *Radical Street Peformance: An International Anthology*. Routledge London/New York, 1998, pp. 38-41, p. 41.
7. Kathy O'Dell, 'Displacing the Haptic: Performance Art, the Photographic Document and the 1970s', in *Performance Research 2 (1)*, Routledge, London/New York, 1997, p. 75.
8. *Ibid* p. 80.
9. Marta Kuzma, 'In the age of political reproduction', *Flash Art*, October, 2005, p. 71.
10. Recent acquisitions by institutions include the Pace Wildenstein Gallery's purchase of Robert McElroy's private photo archive, the cooperation between Peter Moore's archive and the Sonnabend Gallery, the handling of the Allan Kaprow estate by the Galerie Hauser and Wirth and, for example, the acquisition of the entire image and press archive of Viennese Actionism by the Museum Moderner Kunst Stiftung Ludwig in Vienna.
11. See, for example, Claire Bishop, 'Antagonism and Relational Aesthetics', *OCTOBER* 110, Fall 2004, pp. 51–79; or Anna Dezeuze, 'Everyday life, "relational aesthetics" and the "transfiguration of the commonplace"', *Journal of Visual Art Practice 5 no. 3*, 2006, pp. 143–52.
12. *In the near future* first took place in 2005 in New York City.
13. Jaques Rancière, 'The Emancipated Spectator', *Artforum*, March 2007, p. 280.
14. *Ibid.*

Rosemary Mayer and Alice Maude-Roxby

*The immediacy of the artist's presence as artwork/catalysis confronts
the viewer with a broader, more powerful, and more ambiguous situation
than discrete forms or objects. For example,* Catalysis IV, *in which I
dressed very conservatively but stuffed a large white bath towel into the
sides of my mouth until my cheeks bulged to about twice their normal
size, letting the rest of it hang down my front and riding the bus, subway,
and Empire State Building elevator;* Catalysis VI *in which I attached
helium-filled Mickey Mouse balloons from each of my ears, under my
nose, to my two front teeth, and from thin strands of my hair, then
walked through Central Park and the lobby of the Plaza Hotel, and rode
the subway during morning rush hour.*[1]

Adrian Piper

I know Adrian Piper's Catalysis IV, 1970, *through two black and white photographs that I have seen in publications. In one photograph Piper is seen on the left-hand side of the frame, with bulging cheeks and a white towel spilling from her mouth. Piper is photographed on a bus. Two women are seated next to her, one of whom faces away and seems to intentionally ignore her. The right-hand edge of the photograph crops through the face of the other woman who is caught surreptitiously glancing across at Piper. The photograph seems to capture the process through which the two women take in, assimilate, judge, and react to Piper's presence. In considering the image it would seem that the conclusive act of artist Rosemary Mayer photographing their participation, may have been extremely provocative.*

Rosemary Mayer is an artist and writer, her reviews and articles, including writing on Piper's work, were regularly published in

Arts Magazine in the 1970s. The following correspondence took place via post in April 2007.

ALICE MAUDE-ROXBY: Could you tell me how you came to photograph Adrian Piper's performances in the early 1970s and about your experience of the work?

ROSEMARY MAYER: Adrian and I were art school friends. When she began doing performance, I offered to photograph as a friend helping a friend.

The New York City streets were very different in the 1970s than they are today. The streets were truly 'mean' and the atmosphere taut. When Adrian performed, people stared, either with stiff blank faces or open hostility. I think today New Yorkers would simply smile, and perhaps ask questions. Because of this atmosphere, photographing Adrian's performances was somewhat nerve-wracking. I felt I had to get

Rosemary Mayer, *Spell*, 1978.

it right, right there on the spot. No mistakes. I wanted to show Adrian's actions and include enough background to show the scene. If I remember correctly I shot entire rolls of film and had contact sheets made. We must have chosen the best shots. I suspect Adrian has the negatives and contact sheets.

AMR: I am very interested in your writing, in particular 'Performance and Experience', the article published in the Dec–Jan 1973 issue of *Arts Magazine*. You examine the interface between life experiences and performances by Adrian Piper, Vito Acconci, and Terry Fox. In her book *Out of Order, Out of Sight*, Piper includes 'Kinds of Performing Objects I Have Been: Notes for Rosemary Mayer's Performance and Experience', which relates to your essay. I wonder whether this investigation into the utilisation of lived experience as subject for performance was an important area of your practice at that time, one that expanded past writing that particular essay? Does this relate to your taking photographs of performance?

RM: Though it is hard to conceive of today, in 1972 to '73 there was a strong prejudice in the art world toward the idea that real life should influence art. Since I knew Adrian and Vito well, I could see clear connections between their work and their life experiences, as I wrote. Was that idea important to me at that time, in the early to mid-1970s? No, but later parts of my past became subject matter for *Spell* and *Some Days in April*, two balloon works which I saw as fleeting memorial tributes to my short-lived family, my parents, aunts and uncles, and cousins.

Adrian Piper, *Catalysis IV*, 1970, © Adrian Piper Research Archive/Collection Thomas Erben. Two photographs by Rosemary Mayer.

AMR: Your work has been very diverse, including making objects, temporary site-specific pieces, performances and writing. Could you tell me in particular about the site-specific piece *Snow People*?

Rosemary Mayer, *Snow People*, 1979, sixteen figures, life-size, from snow, Lenox Library Garden, Lenox, Massachusetts.

RM: *Snow People* followed the balloon works, which were evanescent works for lost individuals: nothing was left of even the places they once inhabited. I often visited my sister, the poet Bernadette Mayer, who had been living in Lenox, Massachusetts, for several years. Here was a place that had remained the same for so long: the same buildings and the same families, so different from my own experience. I thought about all those lives in the same place, all those individuals with the same names. Out of this came *Snow People*, another temporary memorial but of different circumstances.

Footnotes

1. Adrian Piper, 'Concretized Ideas I've Been Working Around', January 1971, published in *Out of Order, Out of Sight*, Volume 1, Cambridge, Massachusetts, London, England, MIT Press, 1996, pp. 42–43.

THE PHOTOGRAPHER AND THE PERFORMER

Stuart Brisley
June 2007

Art performance doesn't sit easily in the frame of the visual arts. It expresses complementary energies awkwardly by remaining tangential to the central canons of visual art. It is made more complex by intervening in the other arts, e.g., literature, music, dance, etc.

Art performance is the one component of the complexion of art where the questions of material production and reification are problematised. However, all art works exist in time. The issue is not one of the ephemeral as opposed to the permanent. Nothing is forever. It is the question of the relative durations of the impermanent. A performance, for example, lives in the moments of its production. A purist approach might accept this condition. But the notorious faculty of memory will take over as a substantial agent of interpretation, to perpetuate, to develop, or to shape shift. Memory is not a stable factor in art or life. The mind is not fully known, the brain itself is so complex as to resist being entirely known scientifically. As we know more so we realise how little we do know. On the face of it photography seems to afford some relief to the dilemma of leaving the consideration of performance to memory, at a price. It is reasonable to try to remain true to the unique event, in regard to truth and authenticity. However even if an experience of performance does stay in memory it is subject to the vagaries of being partial, biased, or prejudiced, and limited. In the course of time, memories shrivel to become paper thin.

The photograph initially enters as an aide memoire. An adjunct which can block the process of selective remembering and crucial forgetting. In practical terms there is a need to have some sort of tangible evidence that such and such did take place, to have records. Once the question is raised the photograph can become an invaluable adjunct to the performance event. Its significant entry as record, as interpretation, offers another dimension. It releases the performance from the tyranny of being held in the time of its revelation. It extends duration and opens the performance to another life albeit one that is different.

Alice Maude-Roxby's initial interest in the subject grew from her fascination with photographs of performer Gina Pane's activities, and an idea that knowing the motivations and processes of the photographer might open up other considerations of the performance. I had been working with photographers since the latter part of the sixties before I came into contact with Leslie Haslam in West Berlin in 1973. I was awarded a

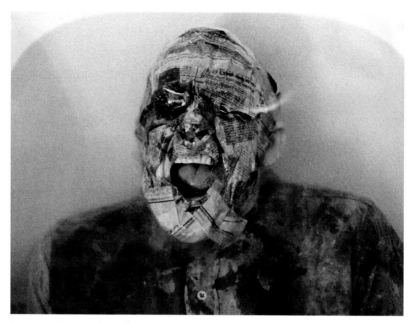

Stuart Brisley, *Bath Works*, 1974, photograph by Leslie Haslam.

DAAD Artists Berlin Fellowship in 1973–74. Leslie had come to West Berlin a few years earlier after two years travel in Central and South America. Prior to that he was living and working in Vancouver. He'd studied graphics in Vancouver and had become proficient as a photographer.

We did a few things together in West Berlin including one of the very few actions made specifically for the camera entitled *Bathworks*. It was apparent from the beginning of our collaborations that Leslie was both amenable to and at the same time had clear ideas as to how performance might be approached through the camera. As our working relationship proceeded other factors came into play which enhanced the role of photographer.

As I came to know Leslie I realised that he was firstly a pragmatist with a stubborn sense of independence even to his own detriment. He was an anti-bourgeois outsider who refused, for example, to subscribe to the usual notions of career development. He was entrepreneurial in a way, in advance of his time. The camera was a tool in some of this but not all of it. He didn't subscribe to any utopian vision of life. His pragmatism was always to the fore, as it had to be to find the means of survival. Towards the end of his relatively short life he established himself as photographer working in the film industry and became financially secure. The last film he worked on was *The Pianist* by Polanski. In a way the financial stability he finally established didn't suit him. Maya Brisley recalls opening a cupboard in his apartment to find a virtual sea of cameras, not unlike her own extensive library. It is reminiscent of the myths told about the abstract expressionists in New York who becoming suddenly wealthy in middle age apparently responded by buying numbers of items of the same commodity. The dream come true, dies.

Leslie's contribution to the work we did together was to accept and participate in most of the aspects of performance. The only thing he didn't do was to perform. And his entrepreneurial tendencies were directed elsewhere. He seemed to enjoy being part of something which didn't subscribe to the tacit imperatives of common sense. The camera was a tool never far from his hands like a third hand. He had a remarkable ability to shrink into anonymity when using the camera. As a performer I was never aware of what he was doing or even where he was even though we would have discussed what he would do to our satisfaction. I couldn't respond in like fashion as there is a large dimension of the unknown in performance. In most of our work together when I looked at the images he had produced I had a strong sense of recognition. He almost always found images which complemented my own sense of what I was doing. Remember, as a performer one is inside the performance in a way working blind while simultaneously aware of the projection, as performance in the making. Latterly we lost that essential connection and the images were less interesting. There are a number of reasons for that. Suffice to say we weren't able to spend time together to find areas of mutual interest and our relationship continued solely on a friendly basis.

Leslie had a range of practical skills and attributes. He was a highly competent carpenter and a good organiser as his business ventures show. Maya Brisley's view of his work with me is informed by her own experience: an understanding of what it means to be foreign, an outsider. Her view of his ability to shrink into anonymity with the camera extends to his life in West Berlin with its surrounding wall, and after the Wall came

Photograph of Leslie Haslam.

Stuart Brisley, *Moments of Decision/Indecision*, Warsaw, 1975, photograph by Leslie Haslam.

down as being typical of the experience of exile in the larger Berlin.

This was complicated by Leslie's own sense of himself. He lived in Germany for thirty or so years and never became a permanent resident. In that sense he didn't formally contribute to the society but was part of its subculture, which is of course to make another kind of contribution. He saw himself as being essentially English in a way, which became increasingly dated because in effect he did not live in England for forty or more years before his untimely death. And while he had no intention of becoming a German national he also didn't seriously consider living in England, or if he did it didn't bear fruit. He was an expatriate for life. This subscription to being assertively English, and living in a temporary fashion permanently in a foreign country confined him and the manner of his thought to a marginality which Maya Brisley asserts is a common experience of exile. He was acutely aware that he was a foreigner. He was in voluntary exile and his idea of home was that of a land he chose not to live in. She also sees that our collaborations offered Leslie a temporary sense of freedom and of belonging. In Maya's view the photographs which were the outcome of Leslie's collaborations with my performances are direct and objective, confirming her view of him as an outsider, or a stray as she described it. The camera acts as a shield or mask. The face is hidden by the machine. The view through the machine is transformed by the intricacies of the lens. It removes the photographer from experience as being part of the scene to one of being outside looking in or looking on. It suggests that the camera in its way is a reflection of the way Leslie Haslam chose to live. I have taken Alice Maude-Roxby's initial interest in the photographer to try to find out what might inform Leslie Haslam's photographs of performances we made together.

Stuart Brisley's account of *Moments of Decision/Indecision,* 1975, as published in *Studio International* v191, January 1976, pp 65–66.

Moments of Decision/Indecision
Gallery Studio, Warsaw, August 1975
Photographer Leslie Haslam

On the first day before the beginning of the work the figure's head was shaved to reduce the sense of personality and to increase the feeling of nakedness. At the beginning of work each day the figure was dressed in a greyish shirt and trousers. As soon as the clothes were covered with paint, and were wet, they were removed. When clothed the figure, although separated by the work, was related to the viewers in the sense that generally he was as they were – dressed in accordance with social requirements. The naked state of the figure induced a more acute sense of distance or separation between the figure and the viewers but a closer relationship between the figure, the wall, the floor, the paint, etc. This sense of distance was required so that a distinction could be made between like circumstances and the circumstances of an art process involving a live person. Bowls of black and white paint were strategically placed on the floor – two bowls of white and black paint placed opposite each other towards the front of the floor area, and two placed towards the wall at the back.

Each day's activity began with the figure placing one foot in black paint, one in white paint, likewise with the hands. This image established the visual contradiction, which was itself a condition of the work, of which there was no final resolution. After the clothes were removed, the sense of involvement in the process increased. When the paint covered the eyes, and the figure was unable to see for the duration of the work, the order of the 'normal' perceptions of space-distance and gravity was subtly changed. The figure demonstrated this limited sense of a 'release' by attempting to climb the wall, as part of the process of painting the wall. No signs were made in paint by the figure: the images that were left on the wall were largely involuntary marks, made by bodily contact and by chance.

The collaborator (Haslam) photographed the work at intervals using flashlight, which also gave a repetitive rhythm to the process. He directed the blind figure, on request, to the front, back and middle of the space, and to the bowls of black and white paint placed on the floor. The collaborator became the eyes of the figure. The figure sensed the space and distances in which the action took place, in order to change and develop the work. He moved between the floor and the wall, from the floor onto the wall, to the floor, between the black and white areas in the space, from black into white and from white into black. He changed black areas into white areas, white areas into black areas and was himself changed from white into black into grey at regular intervals.

In this work a series of paradoxical situations established themselves. The resolution could only take place within those people who came to see it. Given the fact that *Moments of Decision/Indecision* Warsaw only existed in the time/space in which it took place; in order to extend the work beyond that time/space, it was necessary to obtain information and material from the process. The form of information needed (in this case photography) required the collaboration of another person. Such a person should have a specific understanding of the nature of the activity, and be independent in terms of his own abilities to be able to make clear decisions in relation to the work in process. The activity itself changes from one state of reality into another. What is revealed through the process of photography are 'moments of decision', selected from the activity by the person using the camera. The long series of changing states of the actual process are termed 'moments of indecision'. The need for collaboration is determined by the notion of the potentiality of a continual process leading from one state of the work to another until the work is finally resolved or dies, e.g., action – photography – film – book. It generates a democratic situation in which there is an interchange of responsibility leading to the resolution of the work in its various forms. This notion of a democratic collaboration is a creative aspect of the process, and is influential in determining the form, feeling and outcome of the original concept.

ACTIONS AND ACTIVISM

Lisa Kahane and Alice Maude-Roxby
May 2006

ALICE MAUDE-ROXBY: I first came across your name credited to photographs of Charlotte Moorman and Carolee Schneemann.

LISA KAHANE: I met them both through the writers Ken Friedman and Peter Frank, who are friends of mine. I was just beginning to work professionally as a photographer, rather than doing it for my own pleasure.

AMR: You subsequently photographed a lot of Fluxus works. I have seen single photographs published of these pieces, and I wonder whether these were selected from a more extensive documentation or whether you intended that the action be read through a single image?

LK: Yes, there are other images, but sometimes one photo tells the story. A lot of those pieces are about one gesture, like Larry Miller's piece with a finger ascending very slowly from the ceiling towards the piano keyboard, or Phil Corner underneath a grand piano trying to move it with his back. I did a good job of capturing the moment, but the moment was there to catch!

I photographed the Fluxus works because it was fun–so much of what I do is so serious–and a photo really gets the metaphor of the piece. It counterbalances my cynicism about the art world. I'm more interested in context and what art means in society, what role it plays. I call myself a documentary photographer. I follow stories I find relevant.

I think of photographic images as information, material to be reassembled when needed. I work mostly for reproduction rather than exhibition, so in the old days it was 8 by 10s, and now it's digital files.

I like to see art pushed into other contexts. In the late 1970s and early '80s I worked in a storefront gallery in the Bronx. The Bronx was still burning when we started working there. The gallery, Fashion Moda, interfaced with the street literally–the windows could be taken out. Stefan Eins was the person who conceptualised Fashion Moda. He found a trashed out store, cleaned it up and wrote the word *fashion* in four languages over the door. Artists would come up from downtown and mix with artists from the Bronx. A rebirth of hip-hop culture was going on and the two collided, combining a more vernacular art with studio work. We had a great time in the Bronx!

AMR: Did you participate with Fashion Moda specifically as a photographer?

LK: Yes, I wanted to photograph the South Bronx. Working alone could have been quite scary so I was glad to have a frame of reference when people questioned me. Everyone in the neighbourhood knew the Moda. I have a pretty extensive archive. At Fashion Moda, there was a little bit of everything. People would walk in the door and ask, 'What's this going to be?' They'd see this big empty space in a commercial district with some paintings on the wall or a cardboard construction. That openness was

Uwe Mengel, *Woman in the Window*, Fashion Moda, 1983, photograph © Lisa Kahane.

really great: imagine running into a gallery and wondering 'What's this going to be?'

Jane Dickson's installation was fantastic, one of the most successful. She filled the whole of the space with a cardboard maze, decorated with spray paint by kids who didn't yet realise they were artists. It got so crazy one door had to be closed because the kids would run in, run through the maze, and run out the other door. David Wells did a piece based on Cranach's painting *The Hunt*. He cut out life-size figures and put them out in empty lots. They were very popular. They were all stolen! At another time there was a radio broadcast studio in the basement. In *Woman in the Window*, the theatre piece by Uwe Mengel, a young woman lay in the window as if dead. The audience interviewed the other cast members about the crime. That piece played on the violence inherent in the neighbourhood.

I loved Fashion Moda. It took art world consciousness and transplanted it. It could easily appear to be something it was not.

Some people would say, 'Oh, the social workers, they're up there to teach', but we said, 'No, we're up here to learn.' For me it was about a change of context. Stefan had his own definition of what he wanted the space to be and how it existed for him. But the space drew so much energy, from the downtown community as well as from the South Bronx that it took on a life of its own.

AMR: Your photographs from Fashion Moda are interestingly part of a wider record of social change in the Bronx. Seen in the context of your practice, the performance photographs seem situated in an underlying interest in social issues and in activism. There is a political content to a lot of the photographs you take, for example, I remember seeing your photographs of political demonstrations. One of the photographs showed demonstrators holding placards showing Ana Mendieta's face.

People's Convention, Charlotte Street, 1980, photograph © Lisa Kahane.

LK: That was an important demonstration by the Women's Action Coalition at the opening of the downtown Guggenheim in June 1992, protesting the lack of work by women artists.

I seek out different things at different times. I'm a child of the 1960s; I look for the interface between the intellect, the artistic community, and the political community. I worked in the Bronx in the 80s, in a male dominated environment. After that I was glad to discover a women's group, the Women's Action Coalition, based in the art world. There was a lot of activism around women's issues, which are really everybody's issues, at the time of Clinton's election in '92. Unfortunately, this didn't last. Now you can have over a million women at a demonstration–there were 1,250,000 in Washington in 2004–but it's barely covered in the media, because the emphasis has shifted, the times have changed.

While I was working with the Women's Action Coalition I learned about Women in Black Belgrade. In solidarity with them we held a weekly vigil here in 1993 to draw attention to the rapes in Bosnia. Duston Spear, who had the advanced technology of a fax machine, was communicating with the

women in Belgrade and made three black costumes which women wore at the vigil and when they leafleted around for this action. It's a good metaphor, which has doubtless been used many times by different people.

AMR: The photographs in Yugoslavia show the aftermath of the war and record aspects of the lives of women who have lived through that. Can you expand upon what you refer to as the 'Observer Effect', which seems to link these different areas of your work as a photographer? About how something that is going to be recorded will ultimately change through this documentation?

LK: I often see photographs when I'm walking down the street without a camera. I think 'picture, picture, picture' but I know that the minute the camera comes out the picture changes, because there's always that moment of self-awareness. As soon as you record any act or thought it inevitably changes. I think that's one reason I like old photographs because there are fewer levels of self-consciousness.

AMR: Older photographs that you have taken?

LK: No, really old photographs. I collect 19th-century commercial photography and 19th and early 20th-century snapshots. Not that the sitter was unaware of the camera, but the camera held a different position in society in those days. Having one's picture taken was an event. There are parallels between what I shoot and what I collect. My collection is social history, photographic history, and unknown emotional history. I collect images of women's lives. The artlessness that went into some of those photos is hard to achieve these days. Digital photography and the constant presence of cameras has created a quantum change.

It's the unknown quality inherent in these found photographs that links to my work in Yugoslavia. When I find photos at the flea market, I don't really know what the history is. Sometimes I find a box from one family and I get some intimation of their story, but basically I don't really know. Things are familiar, but unknown. In Eastern Europe histories are also hidden. There is no tradition of memoir the way we know it in the west. We're obsessed with life stories here, but there they will only talk about themselves briefly, 'I'm from Montenegro, I have a sister in ...'. After a few moments they begin talking about the political situation. I think this comes from the fact that communism was so intrusive that creating a space of privacy for oneself was a radical act, and they don't easily breach that.

This photo is of a demonstration choreographed by a theatre director. It was upsetting to be 50 miles from the fighting and to see women lying on the ground. This picture has been published a lot, and it always draws comment but it reinforces the cliché of women as victims. Photography and feminism are hard to balance. The emotional content that makes a good photograph can be upsetting. At the time they'd say 'Don't photograph her, she's crying.' When they saw the images later, they agreed that the pictures were meaningful, but when I photographed women crying they threw me out of the workshop. I guess that's what makes it interesting. You walk the line. I guess I like that line.

In several photographs I took in the former Yugoslavia you see the word *zauzeto* written on houses. It means 'occupied', like a seat is occupied. These houses were occupied by families displaced from what is now another country. What's happened since I took those pictures? I'm not sure. I need to go back.

Women in Black Belgrade, 1994, photograph © Lisa Kahane.

Fashion Moda exterior, 1979, photograph © Lisa Kahane. Posters by Robert Cooney.

DOCUMENTARY DIALECTICS: PERFORMANCE
LOST AND FOUND

Carrie Lambert-Beatty

This essay began in 1999 as a lecture for a panel at the College Art Association's annual conference on "Lost Works of Art," and was then published in a special issue on the topic in Visual Resources *(vol. XVI, no. 3, 2000). The rubric of lost art (other topics included paintings lost to war or theft) provided an interesting if unusual frame for the discussion of performance art – art designed to be lost – since it focused attention on the question of what kind of information could be gleaned from "mere" documentation, and how. In arguing for, and attempting to demonstrate, the value of close looking at performance documents, visual and textual, I hoped in turn to raise questions about just where the historical significance of ephemeral art practices might lie: in the ephemerality, or in its traces? I still believe wholeheartedly in this project, and would only like to note here that it is, of course, to be read as part of an ongoing conversation with the work (and sometimes with the person!) of a remarkable set of scholars, including Jane Blocker, Jennifer Blessing, Barbara Clausen, Amelia Jones, André Lepecki, Kathy O'Dell, Peggy Phelan, Frazer Ward, and many others who have been exploring various aspects of this set of problems over the years.*

Performance has long been understood as a radical art of experience; its dominant characteristic is that to understand it, as the saying goes, you had to be there. When Allan Kaprow, Claes Oldenburg, Robert Whitman and Jim Dine began orchestrating events as artworks in New York in the late 1950s and early 1960s, they called their performances Happenings – the very grammatical tense of that gerund evoking, as Susan Sontag was quick to point out, the stress on the present tense that seemed to be the quintessence of the performance experience.

Histories and theories of "live art" have, accordingly, been written around the *ing*, locating the meaning of performance solely in the vivid moment of its presence; assuming that the radical ephemerality of performance is its very point. In 1958, Kaprow, the artist largely responsible for the Happenings, was also among the first to historicize performance, when he linked live art to the modern painting tradition by comparing his actions to the action painting exemplified by Jackson Pollock.[1] By the 1970s art historians were taking a longer view: RoseLee Goldberg's seminal history of performance reminded contemporary artists of the precedents for live art in Futurist performance, Bauhaus theater, and the Dada cabaret. Others went back even farther in their search for the history of art as performance: to Bernini's designs for holy day processions or to the fireworks spectacles orchestrated by da Vinci (to which list we might now add Proud'hon's design for Napoleon's wedding).[2] Such precedents would seem to offer a reasonable prehistory for 1960s performance. For if the essence of performance is its ephemerality, events like cabarets and fireworks were likewise designed to exist for a brief, vivid moment, then to exist no longer.

But this thinking about performance catches critics in a double bind. On the one hand, because the present tense moment of the performance is taken to be the sum total of the artwork, analyses of past performance must begin with descriptions of that moment, written as if the author were witness to the performance event. On the other hand, the passing of that performance moment, the artwork's extreme ephemerality, is assumed to be the key to its aesthetic meaning and political potential, so writers" own reconstructions of a once-live performance effectively deplete the very meaning they ascribe to it. Writings on performance revive the past performance in their texts even while claiming its passage as its very point.

But performance art can be traced differently. To understand performance art of the past is to grapple with the fact that this art was *designed to be lost*. That is to say, it purposefully aspired to the condition of the lost work of art.

The art works discussed in this "Lost Works of Art" Special Issue have a peculiar status: no longer extant, they continue to signify. Their traces in literature, drawings, or photographs describe a negative space. Documents bracket off a place for the work; its traces hold open a site which is both empty and full of meaning. Indeed, it is the traces of a work in text and image that make it a "lost work of art." Without them, the artwork would simply be lost. A Special Issue on the lost work of art is thus also a panel on the traces of art. And it thereby suggests how we might shift the way we talk about at least some performance art of the past. Despite the radical differences between a performance and a painting, a Happening and a building, I want to argue that performances are lost works in very much the same way as Charles Willson Peale's doorway self-portrait: vanished, but not without a trace. Performances of the 1960s are lost only – and precisely – insofar as *lost* means *documented.*

Let's begin with a year – 1960 – and a place – the Rueben Gallery, a then-new venue on New York's East 3rd Street where the artists associated with Kaprow's Happenings exhibited and performed. But let's resist the urge to recreate that long-extinct gallery, to imagine the anticipatory buzz of the audience, the smell of new paint, the shock of the blackout into which Jim Dine entered the room, one night in November, to begin a performance called *The Car Crash.*

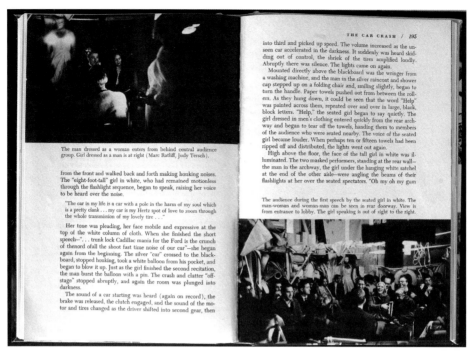

Page layout from *Happenings: An Illustrated Anthology,* by Michael Kirby (1965) showing photographs by Robert R. McElroy.
All photographs by Robert R. McElroy are © Robert R. McElroy/Licensed by VAGA, New York, NY.

Instead, if you will, imagine a faint odour of glue and ink.

Feel the weight in your hands of a small book, on some day in 1965 when you might have encountered *The Car Crash* in Michael Kirby's brand-new book about recent performance.[3] Readers then, as now, might have paused over the section on *The Car Crash*, with its crisp, detailed description by Michael Kirby, and Robert McElroy's beautiful photographs. And well they might. For if, with its nonsense speeches, blackouts, and discontinuous scenes *The Car Crash* is well-known as an icon of the Happenings" scrambled logic, I think it is also a prime example of the way these performances are mixed up with their own documentary traces.

Here is one such trace: Michael Kirby's description of a moment near the end of Dine's performance.

> The man in silver was standing by the blackboard, a large, thick piece of chalk in his hand. With a few quick moves, he drew the outlines of a large car in (perhaps) yellow, then added a window-eye and a huge smiling mouth. As he worked, the soft chalk crumbled and broke, falling on the floor. His heavily made-up face contorted as if with the effort of his drawing, and he uttered a series of noises that sounded as if he were about to say something but could not quite begin a word. [4]

Stripped of engaging vocabulary, illuminating metaphor, or other stylistic nuance, this text aspires to a mode of empirical description; it goes to great lengths to maintain a neutral, accounting-book prose. For instance, although by this point in the text Kirby has already described the engine noises Dine uttered, and the twin beams shining from the two flashlights the artist had taped to his hat, the documentarian refuses to make the interpretive leap that would associate those revving sounds and literalized "headlights" with an automobile, refraining from calling him the "car man" or even "Car," as Dine himself refers to the role in his notes. Instead, in Kirby's text this figure remains simply, descriptively, "the man in silver." This studied empiricism–the facts, and just the facts–creates the effect of distance between the document and the performance; and arm's length between the author and the event he describes.

At the same time, however, the refusal to use the shorthand of "the car" or "car man" to name the main character in Dine's drama works in quite an opposite way. Even as it distances the author from the event, it situates the author–and, by extension, the reader–right in the midst of the performance itself. In Kirby's book, an interview with Dine and the artist's own notes for the piece come just before this description. To avoid the nickname "car" is thus to promise readers that despite Kirby's evident acquaintance with Dine and opportunities to learn about the meaning and background of the work–which is to say, even more importantly, despite the time lag between the 1961 performance and the 1965 description–this particular text is giving us only information we ourselves would have received if we had been there in the audience at the Rueben that night. And this mode has a particular effect. Far from maintaining an empirical distance, the phrase effectively transforms our position from reader to audience member–suggesting that, just maybe, there is a way to experience *Car Crash* without having "been there."

Intentionally or not, Kirby's text opens a door between performance and its documents. Hinged on his studiously neutral prose, performance and documentation are brought into complex interrelations. Take, for instance, that parenthetical "perhaps" in the passage I've quoted: Kirby tells us that, grimacing and grunting at the blackboard, Dine drew "a large car in (perhaps) yellow." This "perhaps," of course, is an admission of a reportorial lapse. Kirby is admitting the imperfection of his memory of the event. As such, the word "perhaps" functions as another reminder of the categorical difference between a performance and its document–an especially important one, since here it is that essential ephemerality of performance art that is at stake. Allowing the color of Dine's chalk to escape him, Kirby assures us that live art will always elude the documentarian's best efforts to press it between his pages.

But, perhaps ... Perhaps even as the confession of imperfect memory affirms the distinction between performance and its traces, it also bridges the gap between them. For surely, if our reporter is scrupulous enough to admit that he may have forgotten the color of Dine's chalk, we can assume he would have told us about any other such lapse. By this one minor slip, every other descriptive detail in the text is bolstered and reconfirmed. It is precisely because of the imperfection of the representation that we can take it as a stand-in for the performance itself.

Returning to Dine at the blackboard, we read that "his heavily made-up face contorted as if with the effort of his drawing." Now Kirby has already described Dine's silver face paint and black eyeliner – we know he has a "heavily made up face." But Kirby has also told us that at the blackboard Dine is creating (or "making up") another face: a car with "a window eye and huge smiling mouth." Kirby's syntax thus subtly collapses Dine's own painted face with the one the artist "makes up." However straight-forward its intention, the phrase "heavily made-up face" is an instance of descriptive undecideability: which of Dine's faces is Kirby describing? The answer, of course, is both: witness the photographs of this moment of the performance, in which the cars' [sic] round profiles do echo the shape of Dine's shower-capped head, and the rapidly-sketched image does, in a sense, "contort."

In the end, it may be this lack of clarity that best represents Dine's project. As art historian Judith Rodenbeck has shown, this performance is centrally concerned with the relation between representation and trauma.[5] I would argue that the linguistic collapse that conflates Dine and his drawing of a car enacts at a textual level the violence inherent in the central image of *Car Crash* itself: the half-man, half-car already being a violent fusion that points to the horrific meeting of body and machine in a wreck. But because in the text Dine, drawing, is collapsed not with a car but with an *image*, the slippage in this passage also performs a fusion of he who represents and that which is represented – a collision, if you will, of action and depiction. Here it might be helpful to know that, as writers on this piece often attest, the *Car Crash* was created after Dine and his family were involved in a traumatic auto accident. This means that at one basic level the *Car Crash* performance was itself an exploration of the problematic of witnessing – of the questions about how an event is experienced and subsequently re-presented that are everywhere at stake in Kirby's text.

Robert McElroy's photographs of *The Car Crash* hinge on the same dualities as Kirby's descriptions. For instance, the image of Dine at the blackboard includes, along with Dine, the out-of-focus heads of a number of audience members. In the manner of Kirby's "(probably)," this point of view admits the contingencies that affect representations of performances, but also suggests that the photographer, like Kirby, was simply another member of the audience. This allows him to become our surrogate as we peer into the performance space. Looking *at* the blackboard image, we are encouraged to look *through* it; to imagine that we too are sitting in the second row of spectators, craning around this blond man's head to get a view of Dine at the chalkboard.

Indeed, more than Dine's action, viewing itself seems to be the subject

Jim Dine, *The Car Crash*, 1960. Photograph by Robert R.McElroy.
All photographs by Robert R. McElroy are © Robert R. McElroy/Licensed by VAGA,
New York, NY.

of McElroy's photograph. Notice the play of eyes in this image. They are everywhere—we note Dine's eyes, furrowed in concentration, and the single eye of a woman seated behind him, which further matches the boldly drawn eye of the car on the blackboard. The woman's eye functions as a sign of attention—again, suggesting the special intensity of "being there" at a performance like this one—as do those of the man in glasses, facing us but aiming his gaze at Dine; the turned, tilted head of the blond man, whose position implies the focus of his gaze; and the partial profile of another man in glasses at the far left of the image. This is a picture of viewing performance art.

And so it is particularly significant that there is not a "naked" eye in the image. Dine's eyes are invisible in his frowning face, indicated only by a wavy dark line that is part shadow and part paint. The eye of the woman peeking out from behind Dine is clearly visible only because it, too, is lined in black make-up. And glasses hide the gaze as much as they signify it. In this image of viewing, there is no sign of unmediated looking. Like Dine's own representations and effacements at the chalkboard, the repeated depictions and erasures of the gaze in this image raise questions concerning the ability of a document to represent the spectacle of performance in anything like the directness claimed by the journalistic style.

Moreover, the erased signs of viewing suggest something about the impossibility of maintaining, even at the event itself, the kind of unmediated contact with the performer's presence that is so often stressed in discussions of performance. This photograph is a sort of meta-image, picturing the mediation and lack of transparency which it itself performs. For as an image of a performance, the photograph is already a trace, a supplement, whose meanings both coincide with and replace whatever meaning was produced in the forever-inaccessible moment of live performance.

Introducing a later collection of performance documents, Michael Kirby would declare that "no written documentation can ever substitute for the actual, unmediated, performance experience"[6]—arguing quite clearly for the conventional assumption that the meaning of a perform-ance is a function of "being there." Documents are but faint echoes of this experience—so many shadows on the wall. And yet, in the same paragraph, with no seeming sense of contradiction, Kirby notes that "If it is a clear, accurate, objective recreation of the performance, the reader will respond to the documentation in much the same way as he would have responded to the performance."[7] As he does, intentionally or not, throughout his documentation of *The Car Crash*, here Kirby ushers in a certain traffic between the moment of performance and the space of documentation. Indeed, the title of this later book indicates just how quickly the door between them could swing: the book's title page reads "The New Theatre/ Performance Documentation,"—two lines, no punctuation—not bothering to specify whether the second half of the phrase modifies the first (mean-ing that this is a book of documents relating to the New Theatre), or whether the two are meant to be understood as equivalents, so that what we are being introduced to here is the new theatre of performance documentation; that is, of the very hybrid fusion of performance and representation, experience and memory, "live art" and post-mortem docu-ment that Kirby had initiated in his description of *The Car Crash*.

While Jim Dine was at his chalkboard, Smithsonian historian Daniel Boorstin was at his desk, writing his book *The Image: A Guide to Pseudo-Events in America*.[8] This bestseller centered on the recognition that, increasingly, "seeing there and hearing there takes the place of being there." It analyzed engineered events like press conferences and presiden-tial debates—events, Boorstin said, that were designed to be represented. Events, by the way, that he called "happenings." Now, it is well-known how Kaprow's term was bastardized in the popular press—everything from parties to fashion shows became known as "happenings." But I'd like to give Boorstin's use of the term a little more thought. Perhaps it indicates the possibility of a rather more dialectical understanding of the relation between performance art and its representations than has been suggested by most critics. For while it has been remembered in terms of ephemeral events we cannot now share—and yet discussed primarily by recreating the live event on the page as if we were doing so—I think it is fair to say that the vitality and immediacy of performance art was matched in the 1960s only by the imperative to document shared by most performance artists.

Descriptions and reviews of performance appeared throughout the 1960s in books and popular magazines, as well as in dance, theatre, and art periodicals. While performances were rarely filmed, photographs of these events were copious. The analysis of one such image has indicated, I hope, how complex many of these visual documents were, and how the problem of performance documentation could be visually theorized within them. But the very existence of this corpus of images already testifies to something other than the radical immediacy presumed for performance art, since photographers dancing around the action at these events would have been reminders to live audiences of those other viewers –viewers like us–who would experience the performance at a remove in space and time.

In February 1967, *LIFE* magazine devoted a cover story to performance-related art, its headline suggesting its approach: "Happenings: the world-wide underground of the arts creates The Other Culture." Attempting to shock readers with its descriptions of "orgiastic" Happenings, the article revels in the "Other Culture," savoring its difference from *Life* readers" workaday world. By my reading of *The Car Crash*, however, I mean to suggest that performance was part of, not other to, the culture of the illustrated weekly; what is strange about performance is not the outrageousness, but the very ubiquity of its modes. For once it is understood on the model of that door swinging between event and representation, performed art can take its place among a variety of 1960s phenomena.

In addition to being the decade of Boorstin's American "guide to pseudo-events," this was the period when Guy Debord was articulating his own, roughly similar observations in France, but turning them to a radical wake-up call for youth living in *The Society of the Spectacle*. This was the time when *New Yorker* television critic Michael Arlen coined the phrase "the living room war," both capturing Boorstin's "seeing there and hearing there," and expressing a growing cultural uncertainty as to whether compelling new modes of media representation made distant horrors seem more real, or less so. This was the time when Marshall McLuhan's *Understanding Media* outlined the structures of media culture for a generation; the time of raging debates about the role of representations not only in describing events, but in determining them, as reporters and photojournalists were charged both with constructing public understanding of a war and influencing policy in it. And it was a time when representational conventions could actually take over perception of the most horribly material experiences: a time when a war correspondent could write home that there were sights in Vietnam "so grim they turned to black and white in your head."[9]

This was a time, all of this goes to say, when tensions between and collusions among distant and/or ephemeral events and their enduring and/or present representations were far from an exclusively avant-gardist concern. This widespread phenomenon provides a context for the patterns we've seen in the documentation of the *Car Crash*. More significantly, however, it suggests the need to reconsider what it was that made performance itself so compelling as a modern art beginning in the early 1960s. Was it the "reality" of the performance, its first-order liveliness, in contrast to the increasingly mediated quality of social and cultural life? Or was it the way these performances, together with their representations, supplemented "being there," in Boorstin's terms, with the traces of "seeing there and hearing there"; the way they endlessly reenacted and reworked the dialectic that was driving the society that produced them?

Though it seems paradoxical, finding performance may actually mean displacing our priority on actuality, "being there," and the present tense. To put interpretive pressure on the documents of performance is not, I hope, to deflect attention from performances themselves, but rather to respect their peculiar operations. Performances of the 1960s *were* ephemeral. To reconstitute them, however lovingly, serves neither their aesthetic aims nor their historical specificity. In performance practices, the accident of the lost work of art is embraced as a mode of artistic production–which is to say that post-facto representation becomes the heart of the body of work. It is as lost–as documented–that performances of the 1960s may now be found.

Footnotes

1. Allan Kaprow, "The Legacy of Jackson Pollock,' *Art News* 57 No. 6 (October 1958), 24–26, 55–57. As many have pointed out, this reading of Pollock derives directly from Harold Rosenberg's description of Pollock's work, in which the practice of painting takes precedence over the completed canvas. More recent accounts, with their emphasis on the index or trace, indicate a way Pollock could be taken as a precedent for performance practices more in line with the concerns of the present essay.

2. Attanasio di Felice, "Renaissance Performance: Notes on Prototypical Artistic Actions in the Age of the Platonic Princes," in *The Art of Performance: A Critical Anthology*, ed. Gregory Battcock and Robert Nickas (New York: E.P. Dutton, 1984).

3. Michael Kirby, *Happenings: An Illustrated Anthology* (New York: E. P. Dutton, 1965), 188.

4. *Ibid.*, 198.

5. Judith F. Rodenbeck, "Car Crash: Imagining Disaster," talk given at College Art Association Annual Conference, Toronto, February 1998.

6. Michael Kirby, ed. "Preface," *The New Theatre: Performance Documentation* (New York: New York University Press, 1974), n.p.

7. *Ibid.*

8. Daniel Boorstin, *The Image: A Guide to Pseudo-Events in America* (New York: Harper & Row, 1964).

9. Michael Herr, *Dispatches* [1968] (New York: Vintage International, 1991). 11.

This essay was previously published in *Visual Resources*, Vol. XVI, pp. 275–285, Harwood Academic Publishers imprint, in 2000. We are grateful to Taylor and Francis Group and Carrie Lambert-Beatty for permitting reprint of this essay. All photographs by Robert R. McElroy are © Robert R. McElroy/Licensed by VAGA, NY.

PERFORMANCE—LIFE—PHOTOGRAPHY

Dona Ann McAdams and Alice Maude-Roxby
April 2006

ALICE MAUDE-ROXBY: I'm aware that your photographic portfolios are very diverse and often involved with social or political issues. How did you get involved with documenting performance?

DONA ANN MCADAMS: I'd been working on a portfolio about nuclear power, photographing nuclear reactors. In 1979, I travelled in Australia. My interest then was in Aboriginal land rights. But while in Australia, I used the darkroom of a photographer named Ponch Hawkes, who was photographing Circus Oz. Her documentation of the circus got me interested in performance photography and the work of Peter Moore gave me permission to pursue it as art.

Soon after I photographed myself and two other women in front of the Turkey Point Nuclear Power Plant in Miami, Florida. This was my first performance: one I set up as a live performance. I learned to juggle to make that photograph (*They're Juggling Our Genes*, 1980).

Beth Lapides first asked me to photograph her performance work in the theatre. Then John Bernd had me take a publicity shot for him at Performance Space 122.

AMR: How do the photographs relate to the actuality of the events they represent?

DAMA: The performance photographs are an interpretation of the events on stage. They are my visceral responses to light, movement and frame. I compose in the camera and interpret

movement and gesture. If I know the artist well enough, I can anticipate what's coming. There's an intimacy. It's a bit like a parade or sporting event; controlled on a small scale and set before me with lights and everything else. I don't really see the work, I respond to it photographically. The disadvantage is, if it's not interesting, you can't leave.

I approach this work as I approach anything I photograph. My goal is to make an interesting photograph. These guidelines were set for me at the San Francisco Art Institute in the mid-1970s. I was fortunate to have amazing photographers as teachers: Hank Wessel and Dennis Hearn. Hank brought in Lee Friedlander and Garry Winogrand as guest artists.

AMR: It's interesting that you've recorded so many performances in the same venue: PS122 in New York. You've photographed works by Karen Finley, Ron Athey, Tim Miller, Holly Hughes. Because you've done this over a long period of time, you must have a real sense of how performance has changed over the past decades: in terms of the work itself, the way space has been utilised, and how the audience has been involved. Have artists' expectations of your photographs also changed? Has your work changed, and how has your process been affected?

DAMA: I've been at PS122 since 1983, 25 years next year. I'm the archivist. Mostly I shoot black and white, but since 2000, I've also used colour slide film. This is a relatively new

Turkey Point Nuclear Power Plant (They're Juggling Our Genes), Miami, Florida. 1980, photograph by Dona Ann McAdams.

John Bernd's Go Go Boys at a Full Moon Show, PS122, 1984, photograph by Dona Ann McAdams.

thing requested by PS122's marketing people. I've always used a 50 mm lens and a Leica M3. The same camera, the same lenses. No tripod, all handheld.

Things have changed enormously since I've worked at PS122. In the old days the theatre was ephemeral. Artists would come and create work specifically for the space, for a community of artists. That changed when it became a black box. Now it's like every other theatre with the exception of two columns, which they would get rid of if they could. It's not necessarily bad that the space changed, but before that PS122 represented a particular time and place. If you look at my work from the late 1980s to the late 1990s, you see a shift: not in how I've photographed, but in how it looks, how I'm shooting and what is being booked.

Holly Hughes used to say that PS122 was a big blonde. The floor had always been blonde wood. Somewhere around the mid 90s they painted it black. I was so upset. It was sad because I no longer had luminosity for light to bounce off. In the early days, windows would be open, so you got natural light and street noise. Some artists incorporated what went on outside into their work. Now the space is sealed off, the audience is seated in a black box. The columns are all that's left of the old PS122 identity. Now I consciously try to get those columns in the frame so viewers knows the piece took place there.

AMR: Does all your work recording performance take place live?

DAMA: That aspect changed too. When the space was renovated and PS122 became the petri dish of downtown art (the toilets were okay, you weren't going to get mugged, it was a proper theatre), the audience changed too. The new audience didn't like me shooting live. Now I shoot at dress rehearsals. But in the earlier days, the work was never ready to go before opening. There were no dress

rehearsals; people didn't even do them. The work had to be shot live. Karen Finley still only does very loose rehearsals. Tim Miller will do a proper dress rehearsal but if I'm there it's for me.

AMR: To what degree do you see your role as collaborative in documenting performance?

DAMA: For the last twenty years, I've been interested in developing a relationship with the subjects I photograph. I've become part of the community. The work needs to be good, and it should also be sensitive and respectful of the artist. I apply that to all my work, not only performance. When I photograph a performer, I'm aware that although I own the copyright for that photograph, it's their intellectual property I'm photographing. It's a collaboration.

AMR: You were very involved with the 1990 NEA Four case. After having been awarded grants by a peer review, four artists you'd photographed (Karen Finley, Holly Hughes, Tim Miller, and John Fleck) had their grants vetoed because the content was considered 'indecent'. They sued for reinstatement of the grants and won in 1993, but that ruling was appealed and advanced to the Supreme Court where they ultimately lost. Your involvement highlights how performances are anchored (often inaccurately) to particularly iconic shots. Could you tell me about your role and experience, and the way the case affected your work?

DAMA: I had photographs of all four of the 'controversial' NEA artists, and the performances for which they were being challenged. This was a tremendous responsibility. It's said that Jesse Helms held my photograph of Karen Finley–the infamous 'chocolate shot'–on the Senate floor. That was my intellectual property, and Karen's work as well. It happened to these four people, but my life was hell. I was hounded by countless press organisations to release sensational photographs. I was offered money, trinkets, diamonds and gold. But I wanted to provide my own propaganda to prolong the life of the NEA, and not play into the hands of right-wing ideologues. The photographs I released were not what the press wanted. Everyone had clothes on. No one looked hysterical. They looked like regular people. The papers had to run these photographs, unhappily for them, because they had no others. In the case of Karen Finley's chocolate shot, it was important that Karen and I decided not to release that photograph. Because it was never released to the media, the photograph has retained its status as a work of art.

AMR: Can you talk about the statement you made earlier about how the editor of a book or curator of an exhibition of Karen Finley's work always wants one particular photo; the chocolate shot? How can you counter people trying to read a performance through one renowned image? If that particular photo isn't representative of the whole piece, what do you do?

DAMA: The chocolate photograph is from a piece by Karen Finley that I shot at the *Saint Valentine's Day Massacre* at the Pyramid in 1988. It was Finley's preparatory performance for *We Keep Our Victims Ready*. The photograph isn't of the proper piece, technically speaking. It was the first time Karen Finley did this piece based on Tawana Brawley. It had to do with abuse and nothing to do with tartiness. But it was what the media wanted. They wanted images supporting accusations the Right made against the arts.

AMR: There seems to be a social aspect; a responsibility particular to your practice as a photographer running through the different bodies of work. Could you tell me about that?

DAMA: I'm not a photojournalist. It takes me years to develop a portfolio. The communities I work in become part of my family. If a publication asks for a photograph of a particular artist, I request whenever possible that the magazine or newspaper send the text to the artist, and the artist give permission before I release photographs. I do this because of the collaborative aspect and the trust between my subjects and me.

AMR: Is there a link running through the performance photographs and the subject matter of the other portfolios? I felt an underlying impetus to photograph things that were not going to be around for much longer; temporary or ephemeral events. This leads to the photographs acting as proof in some cases.

DAMA: Photography is about the moment. We know the moment is always changing, or lost. This is most obvious in live performance and especially performance art: anything can and does happen. The proof of the performance is the documentation. But in my other portfolios, I'm interested in photographing things that disappear: neighbourhoods that change. One portfolio is about the gentrification of Barcelona before the Olympics. I spent four years going back and forth from New York City to Barcelona photographing the Barcelonetta and the Barrio Chino, neighbourhoods most dramatically affected by the building of the Olympic Village. I did the same in the Lower East Side in the early eighties and in Australia in 1979. More recently, I photographed the elders in a small mountain village in Appalachia. The work is called *The Last Country. The Woodcutter's Christmas*, which turned into a book, is also about ephemera, about the trees thrown out just after Christmas that turn into litter and sculpture on the streets of New York City. Currently I'm photographing the life of a racehorse. We know that doesn't last very long.

Karen Finley, The Constant State of Desire, 1987, performance view at P.S 122, photograph by
Dona Ann McAdams.

Tim Miller's Democracy in America, 1985, photograph by Dona Ann McAdams.

Cheerleader UCLA, 1976, photograph by Dona Ann McAdams.

AMR: You seem to have an underlying philosophy regarding what it means to photograph, the relationship of photographer to the photographed, authorship issues inherent within photography. This underlines your references to Erwin Goffman, Diane Arbus, Henri Cartier-Bresson, and Walter Benjamin. Could you expand on this in relation to particular portfolios?

DAMA: There have been a lot of influences in my life, not only photographers, but writers and painters. They have affected ALL my portfolios. My work has been fueled by literary fiction, the way words move across a page, like light on a wall: Virginia Woolf's *The Waves*, early Joan Didion when I was living on the West Coast. Walter Benjamin taught me the importance of the archivist, the importance of looking at and writing about art, about how important narrative is with visual art. About the critic as artist. The work of art in the age of mechanical reproduction, and the importance of 'aura' in a work of art.

You mention Erwin Goffman. Goffman looks at the world through a frame. Everything is a performance. That struck a chord because it is exactly how I see the world. Everything I do and see takes place in a proscenium … everything is a stage. The street and the theatre are the same. And now the racetrack! It's all about them and us. Who's on stage? Who's looking at whom? As a woman I find this profound way of looking at the world, having been the victim of the gaze my whole youthful life. I use the camera to look back, critically, artistically. The incredible work Goffman did about stigma and the mentally ill was hugely important and relevant to my work.

Afterword

AMR: Since our meeting in New York are you still working at PS122?

DAMA: No. The new management is not interested in documentary photography. But I'm photographing a different kind of theatre now. Race horses. I've traded one diva for a different kind! My new stage is an oval, the performers big four-legged beauties. The backstretch is the backstage and Saratoga Race Course is a world of its own, an international galaxy of like-minded people, all there for the same reason: horses. I love it there.

Ute Klophaus, *Goethe's Workroom in his Garden House*, 1999.

BEING AND REMAINING: PHOTOGRAPHY TO JOSEPH BEUYS

Ute Klophaus

The following texts were published by Ute Klophaus in 1986, in the book Sein und Bleiben, Photographien zu Joseph Beuys.[1] *The idiosyncrasies typical of Klophaus' photography and photographic printing methods have become fused to the aesthetics associated with actions and objects by Joseph Beuys, which Klophaus photographed. Frequently she printed these photographs of Beuys in negative, with extreme graininess and a trademark rip down the side of the image. In other photographs Beuys appears in triplicate within the frame of a single image printed from multiple negatives.*

Photographing Beuys was an important episode within Klophaus' practice but still an activity representing only a fraction of her practice. She extensively exhibits and publishes photography. The bodies of work Klophaus has produced often concentrate on a particular location at a particular time. For example, her photographs of Košice, were shot in 1989, right at the end of the existence of the former Czechoslovakia. In the photographs collectively published as Weimar–Ein Mythos,[2] *1999 particular records of the residencies of Goethe and Schiller are seen alongside photographs of the concentration camp at Buchenwald.*

Perhaps what links these apparently diverse bodies of work is an underlying perceptive approach to locations at a time of flux or at a time at which they seem to resonate with a heightened sense of their significance in the present. This mythic and at times almost mystical quality seems characteristic also of the shamanistic quality attributed to Joseph Beuys and his work. Beuys activated objects and spaces to produce intensities of still energy. These manifestations are interpreted and extended through the photographs of Ute Klophaus.*

Why I take photographs

For me photography is an opportunity to look at what lies behind things. Backgrounds are what interest me.

For me, the camera serves no purpose in itself, but I use it to see what is really there.

I am almost never happy with my photographs, as I seldom manage to photograph that which cannot after all be made visible.

I live in a contradiction: anyone who thinks in this way really ought to give up photography straight away, as they will constantly come up against barriers. And yet photography gives those who expose themselves to it the opportunity to think, to speak, to analyse, to capture sensory connections, to seek out backgrounds, to widen horizons in a unique way.

Photography becomes a source of experience.

Why I take photographs of Joseph Beuys

Joseph Beuys is a person who uses his work to seek out backgrounds, capture sensory connections, widen horizons. His language is sculptural, the action, the environment. The sculptures, environments and actions of Joseph Beuys are multi-dimensional. To them

Ute Klophaus, *Crossing the Rheine (Return to the Academy of Art, Dusseldorf)* in which Joseph Beuys was transported across the Rhine in an action by one of his students – Anatol Herzfeld – who had hand carved the boat from wood. 20th October, 1973.

belong time and space. Trivialities are taken out of their normal context and are given a new status; the fixed and the conventional are broken up, given a new context and thereby a new identity.

Both speech and speechlessness are part of Beuys' work.

This is difficult to capture and I use my camera to satisfy my desire to capture it. Even here I come up against barriers. On the one hand I know that I can only capture part of what Beuys is depicting, on the other hand I can use my opportunity to see in order to transcend it.

I consider my work on Joseph Beuys to be original, something which is an expression of myself and at the same time does justice to the body of work of Joseph Beuys.

September 1985

Joseph Beuys and photography

Photography: his adversary

Photography defined him and at the same time gave him the impetus to repeatedly reinvent himself, to escape definition. He did not want to tie himself down and he did not want to allow himself to be tied down. Either he transcended what he saw of himself in the pictures or he walked away from it and followed other paths.

He did not allow himself to be trapped.

He posed for photographers and was, when he posed, absent; his shell was there but he himself was elsewhere.

He never posed for me. I really wanted to photograph him but he constantly prevented me from doing so.

For me, photographing Joseph Beuys was akin to hunting hares. He was vigilant, shook me off, zigzagged. At that moment he saw me as his adversary. At that moment he never wanted to be photographed.

He did not want his secrets to be snatched from him and exposed. He felt that his silence should belong to him and he did not want it to be given speech, and photography is speech.

Beuys always wanted the finished photos.

He wanted to see the result, but forgot that the result is not his result, but the result of the photographer.

Beuys was not a picture hunter.

The photographer uses a medium that he can apply as he wishes.

The medium provides the photographer with opportunities to engage in a process in different ways. Things can be altered, enhanced, left out.

As always the picture emerged and he himself or his work was on the picture and this picture threatened to solidify him, to define him.

He was fluid.

He reinvented himself.

From inside of him came a new silence, new speech, and speechlessness; new actions, new shapes, and new photographs of his new work.

He both needed and rejected photography.

He despised photographers as adversaries to whom one considers oneself superior. Only recently did he begin to appreciate photography himself.

Now he is free and can no longer be photographed.

The hare hunt is over.

The photographs, which no longer refer to the living Beuys, have another significance.

My pictures of him do not capture him. They have never said: that is Beuys. They have always said that Beuys is elsewhere.

Still here and still there.

February 1986

Footnotes

1. Ute Klophaus, *Being and Remaining, Photography to Joseph Beuys,* Germany, Bonner Kunstverein, 1986.
2. Ute Klophaus, *Weimar–A Myth,* Germany, Hatje Cantz, 1999.

Fig. 1 *Music* (1973) Robert Whitman.
Floating: James Barth (performance at The Kitchen).

My first photograph

Fig 2 *Total Recall* (December 1970) Richard Foreman.

MY HISTORY (THE INTRACTABLE)

Reality and Past. The name of Photography's noeme will therefore be:
"That-has-been," or the Intractable.[1]

    ... A paradox: the same century invented History and Photography.
But History is a memory fabricated according to positive formulas, a pure
intellectual discourse which abolishes mythic Time; and the Photograph
is a certain but fugitive testimony; so that everything, today, prepares
our race for this impotence: to be no longer able to conceive duration,
affectively or symbolically.

    And no doubt, the astonishment of "that-has-been" will also disappear.
It has already disappeared: I am one of its last witnesses (a witness of the
Inactual), and this book is its archaic trace.

    ... Such is the Photograph: it cannot say what it let us see.[2]

                Roland Barthes, *Camera Lucida*, (1979)

> If, according to Roland Barthes, photography oscillates between two poles,
> art and the real, I am on the side of the real- at least I was in the years pre-
> ceding the writing of *Camera Lucida*, which was also the time when
> I was the most passionately involved with photography. Looking at my
> past practice and getting pleasure from it ("pleasure is an image"), I know
> that those photographs could not be shot now. They presuppose a rela-
> tion with the real which I have lost. A definite conviction was behind the
> making of those images: a double conviction about the validity of a docu-
> ment, and the need for one.
>
>   Where did that desire to accumulate proof come from? Was it the need
> to bear witness, to document for many, what was seen by too few (only
> five people were there looking at it)? I had to photograph it, to make it
> available for future generations, yes, but for me, it was also a way to *look*
> at what I was photographing. Shoot first, look at it later: I was a true be-
> liever in the transformation of action into perception and thought. I was
> trigger happy. Shoot, shoot, and keep on shooting as a way to comprehend,
> to possess.
>
>   I had no conviction that the photographic document could stand for the
> action itself or communicate a complete meaning. I had a clear sense that
> the final photograph was nothing more than a fragmentation of the action
> itself without much meaning, although I was conflicted there: I felt that

Fig 3 *American Moon* (1960) Robert Whitman.
(photograph taken in April 1976 during the reconstitution of the work).

the photo had to be *true* to the action itself (the play, the dance, the performance). What was that truth? The photo had to project an ideal notion of the aesthetics of the piece: that was my mission. The truth of the photograph lay in not betraying the other, the artist, whose performance piece it was. My only interest in photography lay in measuring myself against another subjectivity, the one that had shaped the performance, dance, theater that I was photographing. I was guessing what that other subjectivity was doing by taking the photographs his or her work deserved. I was interested in the work, not in the photography.

In looking now at those photographs of the past, I can retrace the path of my own subjectivity and measure how much it has changed. I am writing my own history with the artifacts that my compulsive documentation has left behind. In doing so, I am attempting to retrace my education and to uncover the ideology/aesthetics behind the work.

Retroactively, I analyze not one practice, but two. There is one for dance and another for theater. Most dance from the '70s utilizes spatial backdrop as something to erase: the gymnasium should not register, it is not there, or if it is there, it just signifies "ordinariness," "the quotidian," "casualness." The movement, the vocabulary of the choreographer, is what has to be represented. You try to extract and reveal the significance of the movement as well as you can. Your task is one of abstraction. In theater, on the contrary, the space is defined and structured by the staging, and the interaction between body, object and set is more important than movement. You avoid representing movement, which you consider a distraction. Dance is like painting and theater is like sculpture.

Of course, that methodology was strongly inflected by the period in

Fig 4 *Light Touch* (1976) Robert Whitman.

which I started to understand what I was doing, the early to mid '70s.
There is a clear difference between the '70s and the '80s when the an-
titheatrical position of modern dance changed and Trisha Brown's collaboration with Robert Rauschenberg started a new phase in her work.
Obviously, Merce Cunningham had worked with Rauschenberg in the '50s
and later with Jasper Johns in the '60s. But I started to take photographs of
dance in the '70s and it is only through photographs that I knew the early
Cunningham and the Judson era. It is no wonder if I felt, then, that photographs were needed. The continuity between the immediate past (the '60s)
and my present (the '70s, my time as a photographer) was too important.
I don't feel much of a continuum now. This is why, I think, documentary
photography has disappeared, to be replaced by advertising images, which
can still be made from photographs, but increasingly are not.

At the time, I felt the need to remain instinctive and not technical
about what I was doing. While photographing dance versus theater,
I had built different mechanisms for the two different tasks. In any case,
I thought that shooting photographs was an instinctive response to visual
stimuli. The activity was not reasoned. It was not a matter of logic. Here,
I speak of what I felt then. In retrospect, I don't see a lack of logic. On the
contrary, I see a very strong composition inside a frame, which is nothing
but logic. And I feel that I was attracted to the works I photographed
because of their multiple framing devices (Berthold Brecht's influence on
Richard Foreman's theater or Yvonne Rainer's performance). I was also
attracted by their ambiguities, which I could clarify while taking the
photograph, without reducing the photograph to the graphic. Despite
my desire for abstraction, I didn't feel that shooting a movement against

Fig 5 *Light Touch* (1976) Robert Whitman.

seamless white paper worked. It actually transformed the movement into a pose and every pose looked the same.[3] Extracting the body from the tri-dimensionality of the space was not interesting to me. Location shooting was the challenge. I never felt tempted to move my dance or theater photography practice to a studio.

My practice followed certain rules:

1. Try to cover everything. Don't make choices on the spot. Shoot as much as possible – every change, action, and so on. Vary focal length and size, in order to have a choice of scale for certain actions.
2. Editorial decisions must not be made prior to shooting but after shooting, although you want to have some idea of what you are going to do (see rule 4).
3. Be prepared to shoot several rolls of 35 mm film to print maybe only one photo. The contact sheets are what will stand as a record of the piece. Although they will not be published, they are the documentation you value. This practice preceded the illusion of documentation presented by the VHS camcorder.
4. Know the performance before photographing it. Avoid taking pictures without having seen the piece at least once. Shoot the performance several times (on average two or three times).

The practice was labor intensive and became impractical in union theaters when you could only shoot the day before the premiere, at a time when the performers were preoccupied with last minute readjustments to blocking space and lighting cues on an unfamiliar stage.

Being a filmmaker, I was never tempted to go into video documentation (essentially a one camera view in the real time of the performance, which I felt was the negation of any choice). Why watch the performance on video when you could watch the "real thing," or when you could contemplate two or three photographs that would tell you so much more? Nothing can replace the immediacy and punch of just one photograph (as long as it is not reductive). The photograph communicates the presence of the performer's body in a way a video cannot. Does it communicate more?

I am asking myself: was Roland Barthes correct to assume that the photograph cannot say what it allows us to see? Let us look more closely.

One of my favorite photographs

Fig 6 *Sophia = (Wisdom) part 3: The Cliffs* (1972) Richard Foreman.
From left to right: Kate Mannheim, Linda Patton.

Richard Foreman

Everything started for me with Richard Foreman and his Ontological-Hysteric Theater. I photographed every production from *Total Recall* (1970) until *Boulevard de Paris* (1978). The experience taught me how to look.

In retrospect, the photographs misrepresent the system devised by Foreman in his Ontological-Hysteric Theater. Foreman's intent is to create an experiential situation in which the spectator is physically called into engagement with his own mind rather than solicited to project himself and identify with the actor's character, as in a spectacle.

The lights are on us, literally, and we are seen as much as we see.

The system is the one of "direct address": the actors look at us and we look at them.

The photograph, on the contrary, shows only one side of the spatial dynamic produced during the enactment of a play. It shows what the spectator sees of the actor's space, although often the staging is meant to represent the actor's dual world, one in which the imaginary (stage right or upstage) is visualized with the physical (stage left or downstage.) Foreman constructs for us a precise topology, a symbolic, a psychoanalytical reading (a misreading, to be sure.) No critical distance is established or desired: we are put in the middle of a world and can't escape it or dominate it.

Aesthetics is not critical but ontological.

What you see is indeed not what it said.

The play *PAIN(t)* had several unusual characteristics. The main protagonist was not a Foreman's alias, (often named Max), as was the rule in the Ontological Hysteric Theater productions from its inception in 1968. Instead of Max, the protagonist was Rhoda. And Rhoda had a double named Eleanor. The two parts were played by two sisters, Kate and Nora Mannheim. Kate had already become a leading force in Foreman's theater since *Sophia* (1972). Nora never appeared in a Foreman play before or since. The play was performed in rotation, in April and May 1974, with *Vertical Mobility* whose protagonist was Max. The two plays were in total contrast, *PAIN(t)* was all tension about "making art" and *Vertical Mobility* all calm and serenity about "Max, who has given up writing".

At the time, I read *PAIN(t)* as a feminist statement, although a very ambivalent one.[4] I also admired the multiple painterly references and the allegory about the creative process as a battleground against narcissism (a big statement which I am not going to defend or prove, as Richard Foreman would never forgive me, if I tried). Certainly the photographic evidence argues against oversimplification and literal meaning and fiercely resists a single allegorical key.

So everything that follows is a misrepresentation (a very Ontological-Hysteric Theater concept). However intellectual stimulation as well as erotic undercurrents have been key to Foreman's impact. And when "the play is over, you are left with your own thoughts" (as stated in the closing line of the play). Fortunately I am left with photographs as well as thoughts. And I have the published text[5] of the play to play with.

[Lights dim to a single bulb over the spectators. Enter people under white sheets. Music, drums, as people in the very dim light on-stage slowly shift positions.

They appear—more and more hooded figures—who sternly admonish the audience by shaking a warning finger at them. Lights up. All are frozen.]

Figure 7—Two small icons are quickly displayed and disappear. The staging is full of pairs: two icons, two chandeliers, two sisters, two canvases. The space is often cut in two areas, left side for the physical world, right side for the unconscious.

Figure 8—The play starts with a reference to Courbet's *Atelier du peintre*. For me the reference is clear, although I don't know if anyone else sees it. Maybe it is because of the lonely figure of the naked model (Mimi Johnson) in the middle of a studio full of dressed people. But there is a twist: the painter is not turned towards his canvas. The painter is turned

towards us, and lights are shining into our eyes. We are the audience. Are we the canvas?

In the center, Rhoda (Kate Mannheim) confronts Eleanor (Nora Mannheim.) They argue about what it takes to be a great painter:

ELEANOR: How could I get to be a great artist like you, Rhoda?
RHODA: Practice.
ELEANOR: [Pause] With paint?

And later in the scene:
RHODA: Do you think you can paint as good as a man?
ELEANOR: Better. [Pause, then Eleanor rushes to Rhoda and they began to fight.]

Figure 9—Another set (scene 2, countryside according to the published play).

This time the reference for me is Impressionism, or a Jean Renoir movie maybe, because of the fleshy body of Ida, the same naked model[6] seen in scene 1. We see Rhoda comparing herself to Ida.

RHODA: "It is like looking into a mirror. [Pause]

Figure 10 & Figure 11—The word *means* is carried on stage (by Norma Jean Deak) in scene 4, then the word *painter* follows while Rhoda enters with an easel and a *voice* (taped recording of Richard Foreman's voice) is heard:

    VOICE: Oh Rhoda try stuffing the word *painter* into your ass.

    RHODA: It's too big a word.

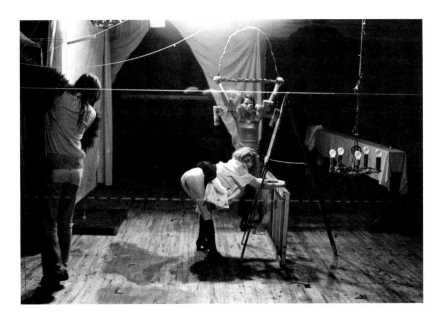

Figure 12 & Figure 13—A crew member (Bob Fleischner) dressed with the white chef's hat obliges Rhoda. Then Max (Stuart Sherman) and another helper (Charles Bergengren) finish the deed while Eleanor arrives and sprays into Rhoda's mouth.

ELEANOR: It is like being an artist isn't it?

RHODA: It is now when I'm ...

ELEANOR: What?

RHODA: [Pause] Thinking.

ALL: Oh Rhoda you are not thinking. Somebody else is thinking.

Figure 14—Eleanor presses her body against Rhoda's body. All my love for baroque painting comes to my rescue. I think about Saint Jerome wrestling with the devil or the martyrdom of Saint Sebastian.

ELEANOR: Maybe we're part of the same body.

RHODA: No, we're different bodies.

Figure 15—Same scene, Eleanor and Rhoda are wrestling in bed while Ida looks on.

Figure 16—The model (Ida) trying to look behind the canvas.

Figure 17—Rhoda reflects with amazement at what appears behind her canvas.

    RHODA: There doesn't seem any longer to be a relation
between my paintbrush and the picture that comes out of it.
(Pause) Try it, huh.
    Meanwhile I see briefly a Cranach with the word *ecstasy* coming and
going and I see Rhoda thinking.

Figure 18—Rhoda has a small painting that is a copy of the bigger painting, behind which, earlier, Ida had tried to look (fig 16).

Rhoda presents to us the same arm gesture seen in scene 1.

RHODA: I wonder if this part was very real.

Figure 19—Rhoda and Eleanor confront us once more.

RHODA: Let's fight; come on let's fight! [Long pause, no movement, then starts to cry.]

Figure 20—Rhoda and Eleanor look at us. It is the last scene (scene 8).

RHODA: Like lightning, every ten seconds I see for a long time.
ELEANOR: Like history.
RHODA: Like a river.
ELEANOR: Like a hole dug.
RHODA: Like mud.

Figure 21—The last action in the play.

VOICE: The play's over. You're left with your own thoughts.
Can you really get interested in them or are they just occurring?

Yvonne Rainer

From Yvonne, I learned how to watch carefully, how to concentrate. Yvonne Rainer is rehearsing *Walk She Said* while Valda Setterfield and Shirley Soffer look on (fig. 22). The photograph was taken on March 19, 1972. It is one of my favorite pictures. I like the sense of informality and the intimacy between Yvonne and Valda. Although the photograph was shot during a rehearsal, the actual performance of the dance had the same informality, which reflected the performers' complicity in the choreographer's refusal of dance as spectacle. No undue ornament or inflated gestures, an aesthetics of the ordinary, the banal.

The photograph was taken by accident. I was there to prepare for the shooting of Yvonne's film *Lives of Performers*, which was shot the following month. All through the '70s, I prepared my film work (as director of photography or filmmaker) by taking photographs as a way to feel the subject, the space, and, in this case the movement and the interaction between people. I valued the way in which taking photographs helped to incorporate instinctive responses into the creative process. I was searching for John Cage's golden rule of chance. In no way was the photograph meant as a draft for a shot to be filmed later. Photography was used as a tool, not an end product. I certainly was not alone in using photography for its immediacy.

From the same series, Yvonne is in the box trying out something while Valda looks on (fig. 23). The photograph evokes a conversation about work rather than a dance. And the photograph makes me privy to the conversation.

At Cape Cod during the shooting of what later will become *Film About a Woman Who ...* Yvonne was gathering footage for her performance *Story About a Woman Who ...* The photograph is a staged family snapshot. The "father" is John Erdman, the "daughter" Sarah Soffer and the "mother" Shirley Soffer. The photograph shows a "staged" vacant look on the parents' faces while the girl is about to rise or throw the ball at us. It was taken September 23, 1973.

Fig 22 *Walk She Said* (1972) Yvonne Rainer.
From left to right: Shirley Soffer, Valda Setterfield, Yvonne Rainer.

Fig 23 *Yvonne and the Box* (1972) Yvonne Rainer.
From left to right: Valda Setterfield, Yvonne Rainer.

Fig 24 *Family Snapshot for Story About a Woman Who ...* (September 1973) Yvonne Rainer.
From left to right: John Erdman, Sarah Soffer and Shirley Soffer.

Fig 25 *Glacial Decoy* (1979) choreography by Trisha Brown and set by Robert Rauschenberg.
From left to right: Trisha Brown, Lisa Kraus.

Trisha Brown

From Trisha, I learned fluidity and speed.

In *Glacial Decoy* (1979), Trisha Brown collaborated with Robert
Rauschenberg who designed set and costumes for the piece. The set
consisted of four huge frames onto which black-and-white slides were
projected. The slides were slowly moving from left to right and the
costumes were transparent. You could see the body through the fabric.
This was the last year that the company was made up only of women.
It was an extraordinary moment in the history of the company and in
Brown's choreography, the year following her break through solo, *Water
Motor*.

  Opal Loop was premiered in a loft in SoHo in June 1980. The dance
performed by four dancers (one man and three women) used a mechanism,
which sent fog behind the dancers as the dance progressed. Fog cannot be
lit from the front, so back light was used to silhouette the dancers against
a changing density of fog. The thrill was in the constant movement of the
light transported through the moving fog as it interacted with the movement of the dancers.

  Lateral Pass was shot in Minneapolis where the piece premiered with
a brilliantly colored set and costumes by Nancy Graves (August and

Fig 26 *Glacial Decoy* (1979) choreography by Trisha Brown and set by Robert Rauschenberg.
From left to right: Nina Lundborg, Elizabeth Valsing, Lisa Kraus.
Fig 27 *Opal Loop* (1980) choreography by Trisha Brown.
In center, Trisha Brown, on the left Lisa Kraus and Stephen Petronio.

Fig 28 *Opal Loop* (1980) choreography by Trisha Brown.
From left to right: Trisha Brown, Eva Karczag, Stephen Petronio, and Lisa Kraus.
Fig 29 *Opal Loop* (1980) choreography by Trisha Brown.
From left to right: Trisha Brown, Stephen Petronio, Eva Karczag, and Lisa Kraus.

September 1985). The set was made of different shapes hung in such a way that the pieces could be moved up and down while the dancers were on stage. You could see dancers moving in front or behind the set pieces, which from afar looked like colored shapes inspired by satellite maps. The costumes were made of saturated pastel colors with transparent and iridescent fabrics. Nancy Graves had great fun in designing whimsical markings on the dancer's leotards. Diane Madden had a classical ballet tutu and Trisha a shining cape straight out of a fairy tale. The dance was a display of virtuosity and athletic moves.

Color had invaded the world of dance, and unlike any of the performances I had shot in the past, I felt that this time shooting in black-and-white was a distortion of what I was seeing. But at the time, the technology of color slides was not tolerant of low exposure and acurate color was not easy to achieve. The maximum speed of the slide film stock was too slow to be able to photograph the quick speed of Trisha Brown's movement. If for an average dance, you shot at f/2 and 1/250 shutter speed, for Trisha, you need 1/500 unless you didn't mind the blur of fast movement.

In the case of *Lateral Pass*, color was such an important element of the work that I did shoot color slides. As I had feared, many of the captured movements were transformed into blurry poses by a slow shutter speed.

Having resisted the idea of the pose in dance photography during the whole time of my love affair with dance, I felt that color was forcing me into shooting photographs I did not like. That was the beginning of my disinterest in photographing dance. *Lateral Pass* was one of my last attempts.

I am still a dance aficionado and go to dance concerts as much as I can but have stopped photographing them.

Babette Mangolte © 1998

Afterword to My History (The Intractable)
Looking at my archives I am struck by my evolving practice. There are three distinct periods, the first and very rich one from 1970 till 1973 or so, when I was experimenting and trying everything; the brilliant one that goes till around 1977, when I am done with the making of *Film Portrait*, in which I examined my photo practice; and the last phase that continued on and off until my last performance photographs in 1986, when I am treading water and afraid to repeat myself. The shift occurred with the self-reflexivity that came with making a film about myself between 1976 and 1977. This was *Film Portrait* that I finalized under a title combining French and English, *The Camera: Je, La Camera: I.*

Photography, for me, was more a tool than a vocation. It helped me think my films. My first impulse was always to cover the action of the dance, the performance, or the play by a succession of shots, which is what

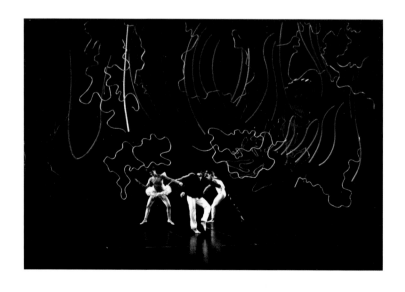

you do in a film. I was interested to photograph in order to understand what was there, rather than to deliver good photographs. I distrusted the concept of the 'good photograph'. I only thought in terms of series. And I thought in terms of a record, what should be kept of what I see today before it is gone. I felt my photographs would help write a history of what and how I was seeing.

I shot photographs because I felt I could learn from what I was photographing. Learn how to see, learn what had been there. In a way, I feel now that I stopped taking photographs when I saw that the subject I was photographing was too familiar to me. I needed the excitement of the new, the thrill of something I couldn't fully understand. I believe now that I needed to feel naïve and non-judgmental in front of what I was photographing. If a photograph is used to pass judgment on what one sees, the photograph is stale like withered flowers. Intuition has to be your guide. If you are left with your intellect, it is better to stop and do something else.

Shooting photographs requires improvisation, daring, and immediacy. Those qualities are the opposite of what you need for filmmaking where long term planning and a conceptual grasp of what you want to do are all important. Unlike photography, filmmaking is not primarily a reaction to an event. As a photographer I wanted to be fresh, uncontrolled and free of preconceptions. In many ways being both a photographer and a filmmaker is a schizophrenic activity. Filmmaking requires control and foresight, while photography requires freedom of thought and breaking the rules.

I consider my art practice as evolving as my perception changes. At the core is my eye, and I am an experimentalist at heart. I detest repeating what I have already done once.

Babette Mangolte May 2007
All photographs are copyrighted by Babette Mangolte

Opposite:
Fig 30 *Lateral Pass* (1985) choreography by Trisha Brown, set by Nancy Graves.
From left to right: Diane Madden, Irene Hultman, Vicky Shick, Randy Warshaw, Stephen Petronio.
Fig 31 *Lateral Pass* (1985) choreography by Trisha Brown, set by Nancy Graves.
From left to right: Diane Madden, Irene Hultman, Vicky Shick, Randy Warshaw, Stephen Petronio.
Fig 32 *Lateral Pass* (1985) choreography by Trisha Brown, set by Nancy Graves.
From left to right: Diane Madden, Randy Warshow, Lance Gries.
All photographs are copyright by Babette Mangolte.
Babette Mangolte © 1998.

Footnotes

1. "Intractable" translates *"L'Intraitable,"* meaning "uncompromising" and "inflexible," but also "intraitable" as in *"traitement de texte"* meaning text analysis. *"Intractabilis"* in Latin means *"irrepresentable"* in French or "what can not be represented" in English.

2. Roland Barthes *Camera Lucida, Reflections on Photography* (La Chambre Claire),1980 Editions du Seuil, France.

3. In the historical context of modern dance, pose and movement are seen as antagonistic. Pose is linked to ballet. Ballet evolved its language from position or pose. They are highly codified, although pose is renewable by the modern sensibility of someone like George Balanchine, who advocated the storyless and nonnarrative ballet. A photograph of ballet always evokes a pose. Indeed in spite of my devotion to Balanchine's choreography, no photograph of his dances seems to be able to convey for me the sense of his movement. But modern dance, from its start with Isadora Duncan, advocated free movement. And that movement is based on a free style use of the limbs (ballet is made of straight lines, modern dance is made of curves.) Modern dance calls for a photographic representation that refuses any "decisive moment" that could be constructed as a balletic pose. I am describing here a historically specific conception of modern dance that was still prevalent in the '70s but now, twenty-five years later, has clearly been very much transformed.

   Barthes defines the pose as an "intention" of reading (Barthes, *Camera Lucida, Reflections on Photography*, trans. Richard Howard [New York: Farrar, Straus & Giroux, 1981], p.78). I don't disagree with this definition but I think that the term "pose" can be confusing when used within the context of photographing movement. An examination of the photographs that Barthes selected to illustrate his book, reveals that he favored portraits and painterly subject over images alluding to system of relations, complex images or images of movement.

   Later on, Barthes elaborates further by arguing that the pose allows a confusion between the "Real and the Live" (p. 79). This is exactly what the photographer feels to be the value of what he or she is doing. We, photographers, want the confusion between the "Real and the Live". We strive for it.

4. Clearly the photographs show many of the shifts in point of view that feminism will later advocate and theorize (the subject-model reflecting on his image, the centrality of the body, and so on). The ambiguity of a feminist reading of the play was strikingly evident at the end when the *voice*–the master of the play as well as the one of his male creator, Richard Foreman himself–took over and reestablished authority over Rhoda's world, controlling what we could make of her apparent liberation: pornographic postcards of the two female protagonists Rhoda and Eleanor were sold for a couple of dollars at the end of the play to the willing spectator while they were leaving the theater (The postcards, which I photographed for the play and printed in a fashion evoking Victorian sepia tone and sizes, presented the bodies of the two women as commodities, a no-no for feminist in 1974.) The postcards sold briskly. I had to do several printings.

5. Richard Foreman *Plays and Manifestos*, ed. Kate Davy, (New York: New York University Press, 1976).

6. Nudity is not meant here to be seen as pose. It is in the course of an action. The nude signifies the model, the painter's subject, rather than the body: an interesting contradiction.

We are very grateful to the author and to MIT publishing for permission to reprint this essay, originally published in *OCTOBER*, Vol.86, Autumn, 1998, pp. 82–106.

LAX, 2004

Hugo Glendinning and Adrian Heathfield

The following is an edited section of text from the script of a live event: a conversation between writer Adrian Heathfield and photographer Hugo Glendinning. At the live event projected videos and photographs of both Glendinning's performance documentations and examples of his independent practice variously accompanied, interrupted and illustrated their spoken text. Lax *premiered at Tate Modern and Tate Liverpool in 2004 and was curated by the Live Art Development Agency as part of the* Activations *series.*

ADRIAN HEATHFIELD: I think of you very much as an event photographer. Your photographs have something of the event about them. You must always be working this fine line between being inside and outside of events, being in the full physical and emotional resonance of an event, and standing outside of it looking on, one eye on the record.

HUGO GLENDINNING: I'm often working at events that I would want to attend anyway, and sometimes I have a choice about shooting or not; like the time in the bar in Frankfurt.[1] I was really torn. Then it was between getting very drunk and joining in completely or recording it. Because I was using the camera I knew I was more distant from the event than I would be if I were just there. That hurt. I remember thinking at the time 'I wish I wasn't doing this, but I can't stop myself doing this'. It was an extraordinary evening

and I was distancing myself from it. That was horrible, but now I am really glad I did it. That dilemma is very familiar: sometimes I wish I could just be there and experience it.

AH: When you are shooting an event, having a camera immediately makes you an outsider for the people in the event. They are aware of your role as a recorder and presumably they consciously or unconsciously start to perform for you in particular ways. As a photographer there must be moments that you feel you are changing the event because of your very presence as a recording agent.

HG: That sometimes happens. For some visual artists I work with–Paola Pivi for example–that's why I am there: to be the outsider. So that she can experience the event. See whether it's the thing that she dreamt or imagined. I am the person who has to forego subjectivity and be there in a less present way, step back a bit, make sure I witness it in a more formal capacity.

AH: I have the same ambivalence you just described in relation to thinking itself. It places me outside of the event, standing at a distance, whilst at the same time wanting to be in it.

You have probably learnt very fine ways to put subjects at ease, to finesse situations, to make your act of photography disappear.

HG: That's true. However, I am a big physical presence in any situation and if I stick a

Forced Entertainment, *And on the Thousandth Night ...*, at QEH May 2007. Photograph by Hugo Glendinning.

camera on top of me then I am unavoidably there doing something. I am not one of those little guys who can pretend not to be there – fly on the wall documentary style – I can't hide. Most of the films I make are when I feel that people entirely trust me. They accept my presence in whatever capacity I choose, that's also true of the photographs I make with artists or of anything I do in my studio, portraits, not just the more intimate video work.

AH: There's something else I want to hear you speak about. It concerns what it is that people give to you, and in particular your interest in people giving themselves away; images where the unintended becomes apparent, through mistake or error? What's your relationship to this kind of performance?

HG: If you slice up a performance into so many 125ths of a second fragments, which is what the camera does, you inevitably find

certain moments that seem to be particularly revealing. This is true for 'real life' events as well as performed or staged events. At its most stupid extreme, for example, a blink might become a moment of ecstatic introspection. These moments lie at once inside the event because they happened, but also outside it because they are only visible when observed by the camera. I trawl my photographs for these micro performances, for the unintentional performance where a thought or a feeling has flickered into life, been caught, and is then visible with a clarity almost unimaginable to the viewer experiencing 'real time'.

When it comes to working in real time – on video – it helps to find situations where the performer or subject is not entirely in control of what they are doing, so rehearsals are good, stress is good and drunkenness is very good.

HG: I was thinking about the Sugimoto photos of waxworks that you gave me. They are very beautiful photographs. But he does so little as a photographer: the subjects are already there, and presented to the world as transformations of one kind or another. I am not even certain if he has added anything.

AH: That 'doing so little' interests me, perhaps that's why I gave them to you. The simplicity is complex. It is a very literal, flat approach to a subject, taking a photograph of a waxwork; a representation of a representation of a person. Sugimoto's photos are often about the conversation between secondary things. In this case photography and dummies. Perhaps it's a little like our dialogue, a photographer of performance, talking to a writer on performance. Two different kinds of dummies; stand-ins, secondary people. One would expect the life of the event to be absent. But perhaps it is strangely re-animated here. The very little that Sugimoto does says quite a lot. The photographs are a series, so seeing them is all about our experience of repetition and difference across time. When I look at these images I think that these people are more alive than when I look at the waxwork. So there is a strange reverse affect of representation, you would think that the more you represent something the more dead it becomes. But there's a doubling that creates an excess. Here a dead thing seems to live again.

HG: They *are* representations of life – they are objects.

AH: Well, they are uncanny objects. They are not wholly dead and not wholly alive. We forget that we are like this too – sometimes it's good to be reminded of this fact. In reality waxworks are often animated by a glancing look, when you look them in the eyes they are just waxworks, but it seems that if you scrutinise them through a photograph they live a little again. Photography has a paradoxical relationship to time. The

photograph stops time, and where time stops there is death. But in seeing the photograph, time past is brought back to the present. The present seems richer because of this gift. The photograph gives back time, but it is nonetheless a deadtime. The present is therefore divided, multiple, not one time but many times. Performance also has this capacity to evoke temporal multiplicity, eventhood: when it does not hide its nature as re-iteration, but shows re-iteration as a generative thing. There is always difference in repetition. Sugimoto opens up the question, which I think is often there in your work with performance: does the photograph give life to things, animate and revive them, or does it still, kill and take life?

HG: So that's why you gave me a book of Jeffrey Silverthorne photos. I looked at those *after* I saw the Sugimoto images, and something strange happened to them because of that. In the Sugimoto images I was believing at times that these people were alive. With Silverthorne's morgue shots, even though these were images of actual dead people, the dead people became objects to me, the peopleness of them had evaporated. The Sugimoto photographs confuse the distinctions we make between the alive and the dead.

AH: The waxworks are mostly of historical figures, so their animation is very perturbing in this respect, it is not at all the animation that would be given to them in the showing of documentary material of their lives. Something highly generative happens in the correspondence between two representational forms, in this doubling of reproductions. It's a little like his photographs of films. We think of them as photographs of cinemas of course, because we always want to locate the unknown, but really they are photographs of invisible films. The space which occupies the centre of the frame is not an empty space waiting to be filled, but a space which has already been filled; a space of erasure. The camera's exposure was set to the precise length of the screened film. This is a still whose stillness is in question; what the still image 'holds' is a particular duration, whose visibility is absent in the captured image. Animation and time's succession are evidently obliterated. This erasure of cinematic spectacle takes place in the very site where vision has been excessively practiced, as if it were that excess of looking that causes the erasure of the image. Testament to a culture over-saturated with images. As Sugimoto says,'... this is not simply white light; it is the result of too much information. So too much is nothing which makes sense to me.'[2] The notion of the photograph as an extracted frozen moment is shattered, since the stillness of each image is evidently not of a moment at all, but of a collapsed duration. The still then speaks of its own representational failure, in particular the inability to fully re-present time: this take is no longer an instant at all, but a mutable moment in which there is a multiplicity of times.

At their best, the Silverthorne photos might allow us to do something similar, to project into the space of erasure, to feel its presence in the present.

HG: I don't have to think technically about what the camera is doing, a little at the beginning perhaps, but then it really is an extension of seeing. I am also pretty free from any need to make aesthetic or framing choices at the time, or at least not consciously. I just look at whatever is in front of me and ask 'is this something that I want to see now?'

AH: Is that because the aesthetic choices, like the technical choices, are so well habitualised, that you no longer acknowledge yourself doing them?

HG: I think it's more that I try not to make aesthetic judgements, because that imposes a way of seeing on the event. Why would I? ... I spend a lot of time photographing but not looking through the camera. The very first time I did this with Forced Entertainment's show *Club Of No Regrets* (1993), it was such a relief. Everything worked, and it makes you think why would you ever bother framing anything again. The more you let go of the desire to make something, the better it gets.

Photography is essentially a meaningless medium in all sorts of ways. Not in the way, that you can make it mean anything you want to make it mean. But it's the dumbest form of rendering anything that you can have. You are a writer and if you write you make all sorts of decisions about what is in and out, how you are expressing something. The more meaningless a photograph is for me the better. Yes you make decisions, but those decisions can be improved by being randomised. Photography really lends itself to the absence of thought in the moment of production.

AH: Is that about making photography disappear?

HG: Well, it may be about making me disappear. It's what I want but I know it is impossible.

Also, I am very self-conscious now because the microphone is on, but I don't generally feel self-conscious when I am taking a photograph. I have strategies to remove self-consciousness when I am working. Sometimes when I am shooting a live event I am responding so completely to visual stimulus through the camera, that I have no idea what is actually happening in front of me. If there is a narrative I will not follow it at all. However, on occasions, when I have not been interpreting a performance intellectually, I will suddenly, and sometimes overwhelmingly, feel emotionally involved.

Forced Entertainment, *And on the Thousandth Night ...*, at QEH May 2007. Photograph by Hugo Glendinning.

AH: So what you are describing is really another kind of thinking, it's a mode where doing and thinking merge?

HG: Well, maybe. It's a great displacement activity for me. Since I stopped smoking, at a party, I can't pretend that I am doing something, maybe taking a picture is a good alternative to smoking. It is something to do with your hands. I know that in the past I smoked in order to do something. Maybe it acts in a similar sort of way. You feel that you can disappear with a cigarette.

AH: So photography is really your means to avoid embarrassment.

Footnotes

1. *Frankfurt Bar Songs*, a film by Glendinning of the after-show bar meeting of members of Forced Entertainment and the Richard Maxwell Company and their audience after their collaborative participation in *Mousonturm*, Frankfurt, November 2003.
2. Helena Tatay Huici and Lluis Monreal, *Sugimoto*, Spain, Fundacion La Caixa de Pensiones, 1998, p.16.

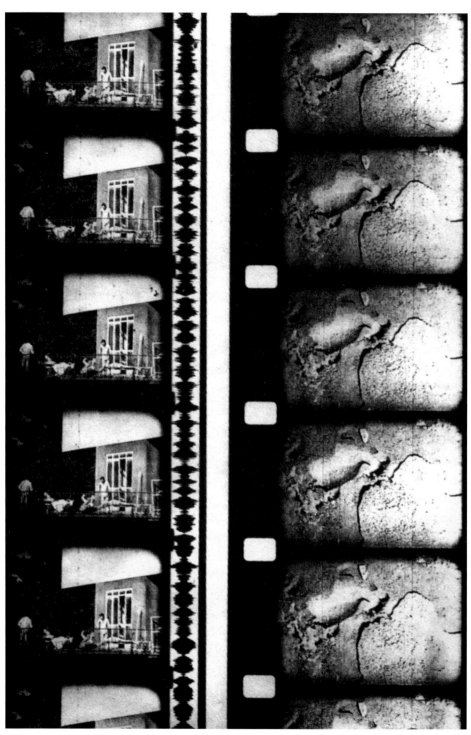

Tomislav Gotovac (now known as Antonio Lauer), *The Forenoon of the Faun*, 1963, 16mm black and white film.

FILM: MARINA ABRAMOVIĆ AND ULAY

Antonio Lauer

Communist Body, Capitalist Body
In a chosen space

Two bodies are arranged differently.
We decide to sleep under a red blanket.
Eleven guests are invited to come fifteen minutes before midnight.
November 30th, 1979
Zoutkeetsgracht 116/118
Amsterdam
Recorded on film by Tomislav Gotovac

Three weeks later we visited the 11 guests.
With their agreement we recorded their
impressions for the film-soundtrack.

Three months later we presented the film to the
11 guests at the place where the performance happened.

Marina Abramović and Ulay

*Antonio Lauer (formerly known as Tomislav Gotovac) filmed Abramović
and Ulay's* Communist Body, Capitalist Body *in November 1979. In his
own practice, since the early 1960s, Lauer has worked extensively both as
radical filmmaker and performance artist.*

ANTONIO LAUER: In September 1979 Wies Smals[1] organised a huge event at De Appel Gallery. This event brought together artists from Poland, Czechoslovakia, Hungary, Serbia, Croatia, Bulgaria. I was one of the artists invited and I took an active part in this artistic event. Marina Abramović and Ulay were also there. For four weeks we were resident and worked on an exhibition and programme of performances. The manifestation of this event came under the title *Works and Words*. At the same time Wies Smals curated Abramović and Ulay's performance *Communist Body, Capitalist Body* (a sleeping piece). Marina asked me to document the event, she asked for the whole performance to be recorded with an 8 mm movie camera. And I did it. Marina prepared the Communist table with food and other things whilst Ulay prepared the Capitalist table with appropriate food and other things such as drinks. Marina instructed me and

Marina Abramović and Ulay, *Communist Body, Capitalist Body*, 1979, filmed by Tomislav Gotovac (now known as Antonio Laure). Photograph appears courtesy of Marina Abramović.

gave me the keys of the loft. She told me that they would undress and go to sleep and after some time I should let the public inside. This would be around 10 or 12 people who were close friends or colleagues of Marina and Ulay. She told me that when all of the people had left the performance space I should lock the door and leave the key so that the sleepers could get out when they woke up in the morning. In the event, all of the visitors left except for Wies Smals. She stayed overnight and lay beside their bed, under their feet.

I am by profession a film director. I studied at the Belgrade Film Academy. I finished that training and I apply all the skills I acquired which are particular to the various roles within film. A camera is my pen. Marina and I had known each other since 1970, she knew my work well and so she asked me to film their performance *Communist Body, Capitalist Body*. From the 8 mm film that I made they selected film stills from which they made photographs. These images, and black and white photographs that I also took for them of a performance where they jumped into one of Amsterdam's canals, wearing worker's suits, or boiler suits were published in their first book.[2]

The Morning of A Faun (1963)
16mm, b&w, sound, 8 min, 24 phot/sec
Director: Tomislav Gotovac
Photography: Vladimir Petek & Tomislav Gotovac
Production: Tomislav Gotovac

One should live self-confidently watching, watching …
The film consists of three sequences- three blocks.
1. The first block is shot with a camera attached to a tripod, while the tripod is attached to the ground, a still shot, through a telephoto lens. The whole block is one scene, but in 2 − 3 places some frames are taken out. Scene: The terrace of the surgical ward of a hospital, one summer morning. The patients are resting, moving about the terrace, joking with each other.
2. The second block is shot with a camera attached to a tripod, and the tripod attached to the ground, zoom forward (from normal lens to telephoto). The whole block is one scene and one shot. Scene: A wall with highly textured plaster, which has fallen off in places, and is swollen in one spot.
3. The third block is shot with a camera, which attached to a tripod, while the tripod is attached to the ground, zoom back and forth countless times, but at different speeds. The whole block is one scene, but consists of countless shots of the same scene, and black and white blocks. Scene: A square with a small chapel and a parked car. A street may be seen before the camera with the odd vehicle passing by (parallel with the surface of the lens). In the background one can also see a street narrowing into the distance along which a few vehicles also pass (vertically on the surface of the lens).

Thus, all three blocks are shot from one camera position each, in the first block the shot is a still one, in the second block is zoom forward and in the third block is zoom back and forth countless times (the focal distance of the lens changes). In the first block the sound is taken from one of the scenes in the film *Vivre sa Vie* by Jean-Luc Godard. In the second block the sound is silence and in the third block the sound is taken from one of the scenes in the film *The Time Machine* by George Pal.

Antonio Lauer (Tomislav Gotovac)

Footnotes
1. From 1975, Wies Smals was the founding director of De Appel Gallery in Amsterdam.
2. Marina Abramović/Ulay, *Relational Work and Detour*, Amsterdam, Netherlands, Idea Books, 1980.

Ute Klophaus, *To the Action Celtic (Kinloch Rannoch), Scottish Symphony, Edinburgh, by Joseph Beuys and Henning Christiansen*, 1970.

Marina Abramović began to work with performance in the early 1970s. From 1976 to 1988 she collaborated with her partner, Ulay. At the Guggenheim Museum, New York, in 2005 she restaged seminal performances including works by Gina Pane and Joseph Beuys. These works were filmed by Babette Mangolte: *Seven Easy Pieces by Marina Abramović,* premiered at the Berlin Film Festival, 2007

Hans Breder is a German-born multimedia artist who moved to New York during the mid-1960s. He is Professor Emeritus of Art and Art History in the University of Iowa. His work has recently been exhibited at the Whitney Museum of American Art and the Mitchell Algus Gallery, New York.

Stuart Brisley has been a central figure within British performance art since the 1960s. His book, *Beyond Reason: Ordure,* was published by Bookworks in 2003, the exhibition *Stuart Brisley: Works 1958–2006,* took place at England & Co, London in 2006.

Barbara Clausen is a curator and art historian based in Vienna. For MUMOK, Vienna, she curated the exhibition *After the Act/ The (Re)Presentation of Performance Art* and the performance series *wieder und wieder: performance appropriated.*

Hollis Frampton (1936–1984) was an American avant-garde filmmaker, photographer, theoretician and a pioneer of digital art.

Hugo Glendinning is well known for his collaborative participation with *Forced Entertainment.* His career extends from fine art collaborations in video and photography through to performance documentation and portraiture. He has also worked as a photographer with prominent British theatre and dance productions.

Gutai was founded in 1954 in Japan and was led by the avant-garde artist Yoshihara Jiro. Other members included Shiraga Kazuo, Shimamoto Shozo, and Tanaka Atsuko. 'Gutai' can be translated as 'embodiment'. Their work is included in *Documenta* 12, Germany, 2007 and Venice Biennale, 2007.

Leslie Haslam photographically recorded Stuart Brisley's performances since the early 1970s. Haslam worked across a range of different photographic conventions including the film industry: notably he was photographer for the film *The Pianist,* 2002 by Polanski.

Adrian Heathfield is a writer and curator. He is Professor of Performance and Visual Culture at Roehampton University, London. He has published extensively on the subject of performance, and he is the author of *Live: art and performance,* 2004, Tate Publishing.

Lisa Kahane has worked as a photographer since 1975, specializing in documentary work and portraiture. Her work is held in the permanent collection of the New York Public Library, the Fales Library at New York University, and the Library of Congress, Washington, D.C. She teaches photography to kids at risk.

Ute Klophaus is a German photographer, whose work includes representations of architectural spaces and cities, often taken at a historical moment or during a period of flux. She is also well known for her compelling photographs of Joseph Beuys's actions of the late 1960s and 1970s. She exhibited at

Tate Modern in 2005, Museum Kunst Palast Dusseldorf in 2006 and the solo exhibition, *Ute Klophaus Aktionsphotographie,* was held at Kunstverein Schwerte, Germany in 2007.

Jennifer Kotter has lived and photographed in New York City since 1982. Following ten years shooting for *The Village Voice,* she maintains her photo documentary archives of performance art while continuing to make art of her own.

Kurt Kren (1929–1998) was a prominent figure in the avant-garde film world, he began making experimental short films of familiar objects (such as walls and trees) yet manipulating them through montage and complex editing. During the mid 1960s he collaborated with Viennese Actionists (namely, Günter Brus and Otto Mühl).

Antonio Lauer (Tomislav Gotovac) is a film director, a conceptual artist and a performer. He is the author of the first happening in Yugoslavia (Zagreb, 1967) as well as the first public streaking (Belgrade, 1971).

Babette Mangolte is an experimental filmmaker who has been living and work-ing in New York since 1972. She is particularly known for her photography of dance, theatre and performances as well as being well known as a radical and independent film-maker. Her film, *Seven Easy Pieces by Marina Abramović,* premiered at the Berlin and London Film Festivals in 2007.

Alice Maude-Roxby is an artist and Course Director of Photography at Kingston University. Her work has been exhibited at England & Co and Galerie Kamm and published by Artwords press and Tate Liverpool.

Rosemary Mayer is an American sculptor, illustrator, art critic and writer who emerged in the mid-1960s. In the 1970s, she photographed some of Adrian Piper's early performances.

Dona Ann McAdams is an American photographer who recorded the downtown New York performance art scene of the 1980s and the 1990s. Her subjects have also included street photography as well as a long term collaborative project with schizophrenic patients in mental wards. *The Performance of Self in Everyday Life: Photographs by Dona Ann McAdams* was exhibited in 2007, at the New York Public Library for the Performing Arts, Lincoln Center, New York.

Fred W. McDarrah was the primary photographer and picture editor at *The Village Voice* throughout the newspaper's first three decades. He created an incomparable visual archive of some of the most iconic images of that era: portraits and scenes from the life and work of Andy Warhol, William de Kooning, John Lennon, Woody Allen, Janis Joplin, Carolee Schneemann and many others.

Robert R. McElroy photographed early New York happenings including works by Jim Dine, Allan Kaprow and Claes Oldenburg. McElroy's evocative photographs were widely published by Allan Kaprow, Michael Kirby and others in the early 1960s. Subsequently he worked for *Newsweek* magazine.

Ana Mendieta (1948–1985) was a Cuban-born artist who immigrated to the United States. She is renowned for her performances and ephemeral, site specific, sculptural works. A major touring retrospective of her work originated from the Hirshhorn Museum and Smithsonian Institution, USA, in 2004.

Peter Moore (1932–1993) was a New York based photographer, acclaimed for his photographs of dance and performance art. In a parallel practice he recorded the gradual destruction of Penn Station, New York and these photographs were published in *The Destruction of Penn Station: Photographs by Peter Moore,* Barbara Moore, Zzdap Publishing, 2001.

Kathy O'Dell is author of the seminal book, *Contract with the Skin, Masochism, Performance Art and the 1970s,* University of Minnesota Press, 1998. Her essays on contemporary art and performance have been published widely. She is Associate Professor and Associate Dean, College of Arts & Sciences, University of Maryland, USA.

Ohtsuji Kiyoji (1923–2001) was a key figure in Japanese avant-garde photography. Influenced by Takiguchi Shuzo (a student of Marcel Duchamp), Ohtsuhi's work ranged from surrealist photographs of objects to reportage. The exhibition *Ohtsuji Kiyoji: Photographs as Collaborations,* was exhibited at the Shoto Museum of Art, Tokyo, in 2007.

Leda Papaconstantinou has made radical and poetic works since the late 1960s, she is one of the first and very few artists to have been engaged with performance and film during the 1970s and 1980s in Greece. Her work is currently the subject of a major exhibition at the Center of Contemporary art, the State Museum of Modern Art, in Thessaloniki, Greece.

Adrian Piper is one of the first American artists to have explored issues of xenophobia and race (amongst other concerns), in conceptual art. Recent solo exhibitions include *The Mythic Being,* The David and Albert Smart Museum, Chicago, 2006 and *Adrian Piper: Actions,* Index- The Swedish Contemporary Art Foundation, Stockholm, 2005.

Tony Ray-Jones (1941–1972) was one of Britain's most renowned photographers. He committed himself to the depiction of the English way of life; at leisure and by the sea. Many of these photographs are compiled in Tony Ray- Jones, *A Day Off: An English Journal* (Thames & Hudson) 1975.

Carolee Schneemann is an American artist, most famous for her seminal performances and multidisciplinary work from the 1960s onwards. Focusing on sexuality, gender and the social construction of the female body, her groundbreaking work has been both highly controversial and influential. Recent solo exhibitions have taken place at P.P.O.W, New York in 2006 and Pierre Menard Gallery, MA in 2007.

Shimamoto Shozo has continued to make performances, mail art and objects since his involvement with *Gutai* in the 1950s. His work is held in the collection of Tate Modern and has been exhibited extensively .

Ulay (Uwe Laysiepen) is a German artist who together with Marina Abramović, from 1976–1988, produced some of the most rigorous performances within the realm of performance art. Amongst others, they explored ego as well as artistic identity. *Ulay life-sized,* was presented at De Appel, Amsterdam in 2000.

Manuel Vason is an Italian-born, London-based photographer. Initially working within the fashion industry, he is well known for his photographs of performance artists. His work was recently exhibited in a solo exhibition at Arnolfini, Bristol, and the book, *Manuel Vason: Encounters,* 2007, is published by Arnolfini.

Marina Abramović and Ulay
Communist Body, Capitalist Body, 1979. 8mm film, 41:40 mins transferred to DVD.
Filmed by Tomislav Gotovac (Antonio Lauer).
Courtesy: Netherlands Media Art Institute, Montevideo/Time Based Arts, Amsterdam.

Hans Breder
Body Sculpture (Culipan), 1973
Body Sculpture (Culipan), 1973
Body Sculpture (La Ventosa), 1973
Body Sculpture (Old Man's Creek), 1971
Body Sculpture (Studio), 1972
Body Sculpture (Studio), 1972
Courtesy Hans Breder.

Stuart Brisley and Leslie Haslam
Photographer / Performer, 2007
DVD, 16:00 mins
Still images by Leslie Haslam
Edited by Dean Brannagan
Produced by Stuart Brisley
Courtesy Stuart Brisley.

Hollis Frampton
Lemon, 1969. 16mm film transferred to DVD, 7:30mins
Courtesy: LUX, London.

Hugo Glendinning
Forced Entertainment: And on the Thousandth Night …
QEH May 2007

C-type prints
Sleeping Louis, 2007 DVD
Courtesy Hugo Glendinning.

Hugo Glendinning and Tim Etchells,
Empty Stages, 2007 DVD
Courtesy Hugo Glendinning and Tim Etchells.

Gutai Art Association
Outdoor Gutai Art Exhibition 1956
8mm film, 5:53 mins
The 2nd Gutai Art Exhibition 1956
8mm film, 3:58 mins
Gutai Art on Stage 1957.
8mm film 8:57 mins
All films transferred to DVD.
Courtesy Ashiya City Museum of Art & History
© former members of the Gutai Art Association.

Gutai Art Association
Reporters from the American Life magazine photographing Gutai group members participating in the "One-Day-Only Outdoor Exhibition (Ruins Exhibition)" at the Yoshihara Oil Mill Nishinomiya Refinery, April 1956
6 Black and white photographs.
Photographer unknown. © Former members of the Gutai Art Association.
Courtesy: Ashiya City Museum of Art & History, Ashiya, Japan.

Lisa Kahane
Performance in the South Bronx, 1979–1983, 2007
Print.
Courtesy Lisa Kahane, NYC.

Ute Klophaus
To the Action Celtic (Kinloch Rannoch), Scottish Symphony, Edinburgh, by Joseph Beuys and Henning Christiansen. 1970
Black and white photographs.
Courtesy Ute Klophaus, Wuppertal.

Ute Klophaus
Weimar–A Myth, 1999, from the series originally exhibited as *Weimar 1999–Culture City of Europe*.
The window of Goethe's house with a view of Juno.
Goethe's death room.
Victory goddess in Goethe's house.
The desk in Goethe's work room with his 'sitzbock'.
Goethe's work room in his garden house.
Juno room in Goethe's house.
Goethe's house at Frauenplatz.
Path through Ilm Park.
Goethe's life-mask, cast by Carl Gottlieb Weisser on 16th October 1807.
Black and white photographs.
Courtesy Ute Klophaus, Wuppertal.

Jennifer Kotter
Schneemann Studio, New Paltz, NY, 2006. Colour digital photo text composite containing interview: Carolee Schneemann and Alice Maude-Roxby. Designed by Sarah Backhouse. Photographs © Jennifer Kotter.

Kurt Kren
3/60 Baume im Herbst, 1960. 16mm transferred to DVD, 5:03 mins
10B/65 Silber-Aktion Brus, 1965. 16mm transferred to DVD, 2:34 mins.
Courtesy LUX, London.

Antonio Lauer (formerly known as Tomislav Gotovac)
The Forenoon of the Faun, 1963
16mm black and white film transferred to DVD, 8:24 mins
Courtesy Antonio Lauer.

Babette Mangolte
Looking and Touching, 2007
Photo and film installation. Documenting work by Yvonne Rainer, Trisha Brown, Robert Whitman, Richard Foreman, and Lucinda Childs.
Courtesy Babette Mangolte.

Rosemary Mayer
Snow People, 1979
10 black and white photographs and text.
Courtesy Rosemary Mayer.

Dona Ann McAdams
Gay Pride, NYC, 1989
Turkey Point Nuclear Power Plant, Miami, Florida, 1980
Shriner Parade, San Francisco, 1976
Tim Miller's Democracy in America Tour, California, 1985
Cheerleader, UCLA, 1976
Karen Finley: St Valentine's Massacre, The Pyramid Club, 1989
Meredith Monk: Volcano Songs, PS122, 1994
Cardinal Cook's Funeral, NYC, 1983
Creative Time's Art on the Beach, NYC, 1979
Courtesy Dona Ann McAdams.

Fred W.McDarrah
Carolee Schneemann's Meat Joy, 1964
Susan Sontag in a draft protest gets arrested at the Whitehall Street Army Recruiting Center, December 5th 1967
A drag queen beauty pageant at Town Hall, February 20th 1967
Wallace, Humphrey, Nixon subject of Yayoi Kusama's election day performance in front of Board of Elections, November 3rd 1968
Grace Paley leads a march against the war, March 19th 1969
Paradise Now by the Living Theatre at the Brooklyn Academy of Music, October 14th 1968
Digital black and white photo

composite designed by Sarah Backhouse. All photographs © Fred W.McDarrah.

Robert R. McElroy
Carolee Schneemann, Meat Joy, 1964
Robert Whitman, Flower, 1963, 3 photographs
Claes Oldenburg, Ironworks/Fotodeath, 1961 2 photographs
Claes Oldenburg at the Green Gallery, New York, 1962, 2 photographs
Digital colour photo-composite. All photographs by Robert R. McElroy are © Robert R. McElroy/Licensed by VAGA, New York, NY.

Ana Mendieta
Untitled (Silueta series), Mexico, August 1976 (Estate print, 1991)
Untitled (Silueta series), Mexico, July 1976 (Estate print 2001)
Bird Transformation, 1972 (Lifetime print)
Courtesy the Estate of the Ana Mendieta Collection and Galerie Lelong, New York.
Untitled (Silueta series), 1977 (Lifetime print)
Courtesy of the Raquelin Mendieta Family Trust and Galerie Lelong, New York.
Untitled, Hotel Principal, Oaxaca, 1973
Courtesy: Collection Hans Breder. Photo-documentation: Hans Breder.

Peter Moore
Wolf Vostell, "YOU", Long

Island, New York, April 1964
Billy Kluver and Andy Warhol with Warhol's silver pillows, New York, 1966
James Lee Byars. "Mile Long Strip". Fifth Avenue, New York, 1968
Otto Piene, "The Proliferation of the Sun". Gate Theater, New York, 1967
Jim McWilliams: Charlotte Moorman performing "The Ultimate Easter Bunny" aka "Candy". The Clocktower, New York, 1973
Allan Kaprow. Preparing Charles Frazier's inflatable building in the happening "Gas" at Amagansett Beach, Long Island, New York, 1966
Six photographs from the series *The Destruction of Penn Station*, 1963–66.
All photographs by Peter Moore are © Estate of Peter Moore/ VAGA, NYC.

Ohtsuji Kiyoji
Shimamoto Shozo, 1956
Tanaka Atsuko's Stage Clothes, 1956 (2 photographs)
Murakami Saburo's Passage, 1956 (3 photographs)
Show Window, 1956
Show Window, 1956
Portrait of the Artist–in Nobuya Abe's Atelier, 1950
Object–in Nobuya Abe's Atelier, 1950
Courtesy Ohtsuji Seiko.

Leda Papaconstantinou
Oh Godard, 1969. 16mm, 4:10 mins
Votive, 1969. 16mm,

4:11 mins
Bite, 1970. 16mm, 2:49 mins
Porn Movie, 1971. 16mm , 0:30 mins
All films transferred to DVD.
Courtesy Leda Papaconstantinou.

Digital composite: text and photographs from works by Leda Papaconstantinou: *Deaf and Dumb*, 1971, photograph by Roy Tunnicliffe, *The Box*, 1981, photograph by Erricos Meliones, *Dim Landscape*, 1982 photograph by Alexis Stamatiadis, *Bouboulitsa's Dream*, 1979, photographs by Dimitris Papadimas, *Oh Godard*, 1969, stills by Leda Papaconstantinou.
Designed by Sarah Backhouse.

Adrian Piper
Catalyis IV, 1970
Courtesy: Collection of Thomas Erben, New York.
2 photographs by Rosemary Mayer.
Mythic Being, 1973. DVD, 8:00 mins (Filmed by Peter Kennedy as part of *Other than Art's Sake*, 1973)
Courtesy: Adrian Piper Research Archive, Berlin.

Tony Ray-Jones
Carolee Schneemann, Meat Joy, 1964
Beachy Head Tripper Boat, 1967
Beauty contest, Southport, Lancashire, 1967
Bournemouth, 1969,
Douglas, Isle of Wight, 1968

Richmond, Surrey, 1969
York Mystery Players, 1969
Digital black and white photo composite designed by Sarah Backhouse. All photographs by Tony Ray-Jones are © NMPFT-Tony Ray-Jones/ Science & Society Picture Library.

Carolee Schneemann
Meat Joy, 1964, 7 photographic panels produced from digital scans of the following list of photographs. Panels designed by Sarah Backhouse.
Interior Scroll, 1975, photograph by Anthony McCall.
Interior Scroll, 1975, photograph by Sally Dixon.
Meat Joy, 1964, photograph by Manfred Schroeder.
Meat Joy, 1964, photographs by Arman.
Meat Joy, 1964, photograph by Charles Rotenberg.
Meat Joy, 1964, photograph by Harold Chapman.
Meat Joy, 1964, photograph by Massal.
Meat Joy, 1964, photograph by Al Giese.
Meat Joy, 1964, photographs by Harvey Zucker.
Courtesy Carolee Schneemann and the photographers.

Manuel Vason
Vitrine display of books:
Manuel Vason, Exposures, 2002, Black Dog Publishers.
Manuel Vason, Encounters, 2007, Arnolfini.